Microsoft Office User Specialist Certification

Do you KNOW ENOUGH to PASS the exam?

Take a FREE online test on the site:

www.moustest.com

Free practice tests are available directly over the Internet at www.moustest.com

Don't leave it to chance!

EXCEL 2000
Expert

Editions ENI

BP 32125
44021 NANTES Cedex 1

Tél. 02.51.80.15.15
Fax 02.51.80.15.16

e-mail : editions@ediENI.COM
http://www.editions-eni.com

Collection directed by Corinne HERVO

MOUS
Excel 2000 Expert

TEMPLATES, WORKBOOKS AND WORKGROUPS

PRINTING AND CONFIGURATION

MACROS

SUMMARY EXERCISES

This book is the ideal tool for an effective preparation of the Excel 2000 Expert exam. The MOUS logo on the cover guarantees that this edition has been approved by Microsoft®. It contains the theoretical information corresponding to all the topics tested in the exam and you can test your knowledge by working through the practice exercises. If you succeed in completing these exercises without any difficulty, you are ready to take your exam. At the end of the book, you can see a list of the Excel 2000 Expert exam objectives, and the number of the lesson and exercise that refer to each of these objectives.

What is the MOUS certification?

The MOUS (Microsoft Office User Specialist) exam gives you the opportunity to obtain a meaningful certification, recognised by Microsoft®, for the Office applications: Word, Excel, Access, PowerPoint, and Outlook. This certification guarantees your level of skill in working with these applications. It can provide a boost to your career ambitions, as it proves that you can use effectively all the features of the Microsoft Office applications and thus offer a high productivity level to your employer. In addition, it is a certain plus when job-seeking: more and more companies require employment candidates to be MOUS certificate holders.

What are the applications concerned?

You can gain MOUS certification in Office 97 applications (Word, Excel, PowerPoint and Access) and in Office 2000 applications (Word, Excel, PowerPoint, Access and Outlook). MOUS exams also exist for Word 7 and Excel 7. Two exam levels are offered for Word 97, Word 2000, Excel 97 and Excel 2000: a Core level (proficiency) and a second Expert level. For PowerPoint 97 and Access 97, only the Expert certification is available. For PowerPoint 2000, Access 2000 and Outlook 2000, only one level of certification is available.

If you obtain the Expert level for Word 97, Excel 97, PowerPoint 97 and Access 97, you are certified as a Master in Office 97. If you obtain the Expert level for Word 2000 and Excel 2000 as well as MOUS certification in PowerPoint 2000, Access 2000 and Outlook 2000, you are certified as a Master in Office 2000.

How do you apply to sit the exams?

To enrol for the exams, you should contact one of the Microsoft Authorized Testing Centers (or ATC). A list of these centres is available online at this address: http://www.mous.net. There is also http://www.mous.edexcel.org.uk specifically for the UK. Make sure you know the version of the Office application for which you wish to obtain the certificate (is it the 97 or 2000 version?).

There is an enrolment fee for each exam.

On the day of the exam, you should carry some form of identification and, if you have already sat a MOUS exam, your ID number.

What happens during the MOUS exam?

During the exam, you will have a computer that you must use to perform a certain number of tasks on the software in question. Each action you perform to carry out these tasks will be tested in order to make sure that you have done correctly what was asked of you. There are no multiple-choice questions and the exam is not a simulation; you work directly in the application (Word, Excel...).

You are allowed no notes, books, pencils or calculators during the exam. You can consult the application help, but you should be careful not to exceed the exam's time limit.

Each exam is timed; it lasts in general between 45 minutes and one hour.

How do you pass the exam?

You must carry out a certain percentage of the required tasks correctly, within the allocated time. This percentage varies depending on the exam.

You will be told your result as soon as you have finished your exam. These results are confidential (the data are coded) and are only made known to the candidate and to Microsoft.

What happens then?

You will receive a Microsoft-approved exam certificate, proving that you hold the specified MOUS (Microsoft Office User Specialist) level.

How this book works

This book is the ideal companion to an effective preparation of the **MOUS Excel 2000 Expert** exam. It is divided into several sections, each containing one or more **chapters**. Each section deals with a specific topic: managing data (named ranges, import/export, data lists…), tools for analysing data (audit, solver, pivot tables), workbook, templates and workgroups, printing and the configuration of the environment, basic principles for working with macros. Each chapter is independent from the others. You can tailor the training to suit you: if you already know how to manage a data list, for example, you can skip this lesson and go straight to the practice exercise for that chapter, then if you feel you need some extra theory, you can look back at the relevant points in the lesson. You can also study the lessons and/or work through the exercises in any order you wish.

At the end of the book, there is an **index** to help you find the explanations for any action, whenever you need them.

From theory...

Each chapter starts with a **lesson** on the theme in question and the lesson is made up of a variable amount of numbered topics. The lesson should supply you with all the theoretical information necessary to acquire that particular skill. Example screens to illustrate the point discussed enhance the lesson and you will also find tips, tricks and remarks to complement the explanations provided.

...To practice

Test your knowledge by working through the **practice exercise** at the end of each chapter: each numbered heading corresponds to an exercise question. A solution to the exercise follows. These exercises are done using the documents on the CD-ROM accompanying the book, that you install on your own computer (to see how, refer to the INSTALLING THE CD-ROM instructions). In addition to the chapter exercises, seven **summary exercises** dealing with each of the section themes are included at the end of the book. The solutions to these exercises appear as documents on the CD-ROM.

All you need to succeed!

When you can complete all the practice exercises without any hesitation or problems, you are ready to sit the MOUS exam. In the table of contents for each chapter, the topics corresponding to a specific exam objective are marked with this symbol: ⊞. At the back of the book, you can also see **the official list of the Excel 2000 Expert exam objectives** and for each of these objectives the corresponding lesson and exercise number.

The layout of this book

This book is laid out in a specific way with special typefaces and symbols so you can find all the information you need quickly and easily:

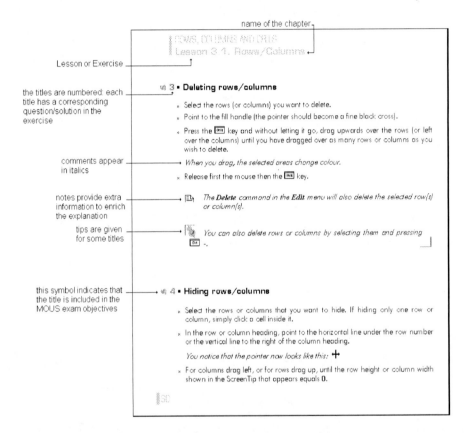

You can tell whether an action should be performed with the mouse, the keyboard or with the menu options by referring to the symbol that introduces each action: 🖱, ⬚ and 🗒.

Installing the CD-ROM

The CD-ROM provided contains the documents used to work through the practice exercises and the summary exercise solutions. When you follow the installation procedure set out below, a folder called MOUS Excel 2000 Expert is created on your hard disk and the CD-ROM documents are decompressed and copied into the created folder. The CD-ROM also contains two templates which you should copy into the Excel Templates folder.

- Put the CD-ROM into the CD-ROM drive of your computer.

- Start the Windows Explorer: click the **Start** button, point to the **Programs** option then click **Windows Explorer**.

- In the left pane of the Explorer window, scroll through the list until the CD-ROM drive icon appears. Click this icon.

  The contents of the CD-ROM appear in the right pane of the Explorer window.

- Double-click the icon of the **MOUS Excel 2000 Expert** folder in the right pane of the Explorer window.

  *The **MOUS Excel 2000 Expert** dialog box appears.*

- Click **Next**.

  The installation application offers to create a folder called MOUS Excel 2000 Expert.

- Modify the proposed folder name if you wish then click **Next**. If several people are going to be doing the practice exercises on the same computer, you should modify the folder name so each person is working on their own copy of the folder.

* Click **Yes** to confirm creating the **MOUS Excel 2000 Expert** folder.

  The installation application decompresses the documents then copies them into the created folder.

* Click **Finish** when the copying process is finished.

  You must now copy the templates into the templates folder used by Excel. The default file path used is C:\Windows\ Application Data\Microsoft\Templates.

* Click the template called **3-1 Expenses sheet.xlt** that you can see in the right pane of the Explorer window. Hold down Ctrl key then click the **Sales by Semester.xlt** template.

  Both templates are now selected.

* Open the **Edit** menu then click the **Copy** option to copy the template into the Windows clipboard.

* If necessary, scroll through the contents of the left pane of the window until you can see the **Windows** folder; click the plus (+) sign to the left of **Windows** in order to see a list of the folders it contains.

  The + sign becomes a - sign.

* Click the + sign to the left of the **Application Data** folder then click the + sign to the left of the **Microsoft** folder then finally click the **Templates** folder.

  By default, the templates are stored in this folder.

* Use the **Edit - Paste** command to copy the contents of the clipboard into the **Templates** folder.

  A dialog box appears while the copy is pasted in.

* When the copy is finished, click the ☒ button on the **Explorer** window to close it.

  You can now put away the CD-ROM and start working on your MOUS exam preparation.

MANAGING DATA
Lesson 1.1: Named ranges

MANAGING DATA
Lesson 1.1: Named ranges

1 ▪ **Naming cells**

A range of cells can be referred to by a name.

First method

▪ Select the range of cells you want to name.

▪ Click the **Name Box** that you can see on the left of the formula bar.

▪ Enter the name that you want to give to the selected cells.

▪ Press ⏎ on the keyboard to confirm.

▪ Select all the cells to which you want to give the same name.

▪ **Insert - Name - Define** or `Ctrl` `F3`

Excel proposes to take the contents of the top left cell as the name of the range. If this cell is blank, Excel proposes the contents of the cell above the range, or to its right.

▪ If you prefer, enter another name for the selected cells.

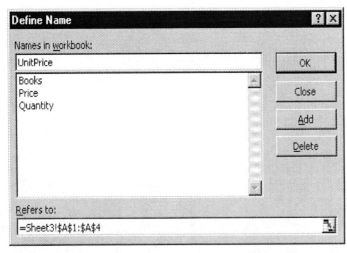

There must be no spaces or hyphens in these names! You can use the button to collapse the dialog box and select cells on the sheet.

▪ Click **Add**.

※ Name any other ranges in the same way then click **OK**.

Second method

This method can be used if the names you are assigning appear next to the cells on the sheet.

※ Select the cells containing the names to be used <u>and</u> the cells you want to name.

※ **Insert - Name - Create** or ⌈Ctrl⌉⌈Shift⌉⌈F3⌉

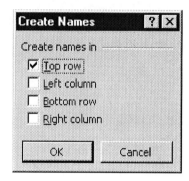

※ Indicate the position of the cells containing the names.

※ Click **OK**.

📄 *Excel converts any spaces or hyphens in the name into an underscore character.*

▣2 ▪ Deleting a name

※ **Insert - Name - Define** or ⌈Ctrl⌉⌈F3⌉

※ Select the name that you wish to delete in the **Names in workbook** list.

※ Click the **Delete** button.

» Click **OK**.

🔲3 ▪ Using names in a formula

Entering a name

» As you are entering the formula, substitute names for cell references.
For example: a formula **=SUM(Sales)** calculates the sum of the values contained in a range named Sales.

Pasting a name

» Start entering the formula then stop where the name is required.

» **Insert - Name - Paste** or F3

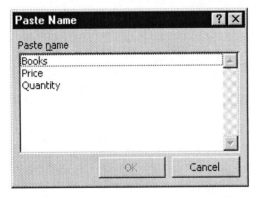

The dialog box lists all the existing names in the workbook.

» Double-click the name you wish to paste.

» Complete the formula.

▥4 ▪ Using **LOOKUP** functions

VLOOKUP function

This function looks for a value in the first column of a table and produces the value found in the cell located on the same row, in the column you have specified.

▪ Create a table grouping together the data that you will subsequently retrieve during your search then sort the table in ascending order by the first column in it.
Name this cell range if you do not wish to select it when creating your calculation formula.

▪ Click the cell where the information retrieved from the table should be displayed.

▪ Create your calculation formula, respecting the following syntax:
=VLOOKUP(lookup_value,table_array,col_index_num)

lookup_value	Is the value the function looks for in the first column of the table.
table_array	Is the table from which the data is to be retrieved. This argument can consist of the reference of a range of cells or the name of a named range.
col_index_num	Is the number of the column in the table (table_array) containing the value that is to be displayed as a result. For example, the first column in the table is column 1.

D14	▼	=	=VLOOKUP(A14,Books,4)	
	A	B	C	D	E

	A	B	C	D	E
12					
13	Book code	Title	Quantity	Sale price	Total
14	BI02	Light a Penny Candle	1	5.99	5.99
15	CO03	Cruel and Unusual	2	5.99	11.98
16	DE06	Way through the Woods	1	5.99	5.99
17	GR01	Client	1	4.99	4.99
18	KI03	Green Mile Compilation	1	7.99	7.99
19					
20					
21				TOTAL AMOUNT DUE	36.94
22					

In this example, the VLOOKUP function looks for the reference of the book (whose code is contained in A14) in a table (named range) called Books and then returns the price of the item located in the fourth column.

▪ Confirm the formula by pressing ⏎.

HLOOKUP function

This function is used to locate a value in the first row of a table, and looks up the value contained in the same column and in the row you specify.

▪ Create a table grouping together all the data you will need to retrieve in your search, then sort the table in ascending order by the data in the first row. To do this, select the table, activate the **Data - Sort** command then click the **Options** button. Activate the **From left to right** then confirm. Check that Excel is going to sort by the first **row** in the table in **Ascending** order then click.
Give this range of cells a name if you do not wish to select it when creating your calculation formula.

▪ Click the cell where you want the information found in the table to be displayed.

▪ Create your calculation formula, respecting the following syntax:
=HLOOKUP(lookup_value,table_array,row_index_num)

lookup_value   Is the value the function looks for in the first row of the table.

table_array   Is the table from which the data is to be retrieved. This argument can be the references of a cell range or a named range.

row_index_num   Is the row number in the table containing the value that should be the serach result. For example, the first row in a table is row 1.

▪ Confirm the formula by pressing ⏎.

Below, you can see **Practice Exercise** 1.1. This exercise is made up of 4 steps. If you do not know how to complete one of the steps, go back to the lesson to refer to the corresponding title. When you have finished, check your work by reading the **Solution** on the next page.

All the steps in this exercise are likely to be tested in the exam.

☞ **Practice Exercise 1.1**

*In order to complete exercise 1.1, you should open workbook **1-1 Invoice.xls** located in the **MOUS Excel 2000 Expert** folder and activate the **Invoice** sheet.*

1. Give the name **Quantity** to cell range **C14** to **C18** and the name **Price** to cell range **D14** to **D18**.

2. Delete the **UnitPrice** name.

3. Use the **Quantity** and **Price** names in a formula to calculate the total for the **BI02** book in cell **E14**.
   Copy this formula into cells **E15** to **E18**.

4. In cell **B14** create a formula that will look for the title of the book that corresponds to the code in cell **A14**. The cell range (**A1** to **D106**) that contains the data from the table is called **Books** and is located in the worksheet also called **Books.**
   Next copy this formula into cells **B15** to **B18**.

If you want to put what you have learnt into practice on a real document, you can work on summary exercise 1 for the MANAGING DATA section, that you can find at the end of this book.

It is often possible to perform a task in several different ways, but here only the quickest solution is presented. Go back to the lesson to see the other techniques that can be used.

 Solution to Exercise 1.1

1. To assign the name QUANTITY to cells C14 to C18, select cells **C14** to **C18**.
   Click the **Name Box** on the formula bar, type **Quantity** then confirm by pressing ⏎.

   To assign the name Price to cells D14 to D18, select cells **D14** to **D18**.
   Click the **Name Box** on the formula bar, type **Price** , then confirm by pressing ⏎.

2. To delete the UnitPrice name, use the **Insert - Name - Define** command and click **UnitPrice** in the **Names in workbook** list then click the **Delete** button.
   Click **OK** to close the **Define Name** dialog box.

3. To use the Quantity and Price names to calculate the total for the BI02 book in cell E14, click cell **E14**.
   Type **=Quantity*Price** then confirm by pressing the ⏎ key.

   To copy this formula into cells E15 to E18, select cell **E14** then drag its fill handle down to cell **E18**.

4. To create a calculation formula in cell B14 to look up the title of the book that corresponds to the code in cell A14, click cell **B14**.
   Type **=VLOOKUP(A14,Books,2)** then confirm by pressing ⏎.

   To copy this formula into cells B15 to B18, select cell **B14** then drag its fill handle down to cell **B18**.

MANAGING DATA
Exercise 1.1: Named ranges

MANAGING DATA
Lesson 1.2: Importing/Exporting

1 ▪ Importing data from a text file

▪ Open the workbook into which you wish to import the text file.

▪ **Data - Get External Data**

▪ Click the **Import Text File** option.

Excel searches for files of the Text Files (.txt) type.*

▪ Select the drive, then the folder in which the text file is stored.

▪ Click the text file in question then the **Import** button.

*The first stage of the **Text Import Wizard** appears:*

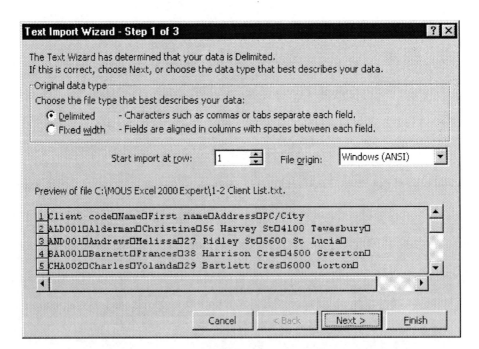

*The wizard tells you whether the data in the text file are **Delimited** (separated with tab stops or commas) or **Fixed width** (separated by spaces).*

- If necessary, modify the **Original data type** in the corresponding frame.

- If you do not want to import the data from the first row in the file, select or enter the required row number in the **Start import at row** text box.

- Click the **Next** button to go on to the next step.

- Select the delimiters contained in data that are **Delimited** or choose the field widths following the instructions in the first frame of the window, if the data are of **Fixed width**.

- Click **Next** to go on to the next step.

- For each column, select the data format. Do this by clicking the column then choosing one of the options in the **Column data format** frame.

- Click the **Finish** button.

- To insert the table in an **Existing worksheet**, activate this option then click the ⬛ button. Access the worksheet then click the first destination cell for the external data. Click the ⬛ button again to restore the dialog box.

  To insert the table into a **New worksheet**, activate the corresponding option.

- Click **OK**.

 The mouse method uses the formula palette. The idea behind this method is to drag the data from the text application towards a Microsoft Excel worksheet.

- Open the application where the text file was created then open the file that contains the text you wish to import.

- Open Excel, if necessary, then open the workbook concerned and activate the worksheet into which you want to import the text.

- Display both application windows on the screen at once. To do this, right-click any empty space on the taskbar and choose either the **Tile Windows Horizontally** or **Tile Windows Vertically** option, depending on how you want the windows to be arranged on screen.

- In the Text application, select the text that you want to import into your Microsoft Excel worksheet.

- Point to the selected text and hold down the ⌨ Ctrl key.

▪ Drag the selection towards the Microsoft Excel sheet, to the place where you want to insert the text.

As you drag, the pointer is accompanied by a plus sign within a rectangle, signifying a copy is being made. If you let go of the Ctrl *key, the plus sign no longer appears: this means you are not copying, but moving the data.*

▪ Release the mouse button then the Ctrl key.

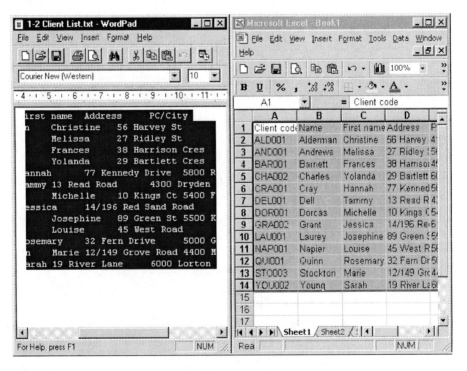

Each item in the text file is inserted in a cell on the worksheet.

⊞2 ▪ Importing data from other applications

Importing data by copying, without establishing a link

▪ Open the application then the file in which the data you want to copy are stored.

▪ Select the data you want to copy.

▪ If you are copying text that is not separated by a delimiter (for example, a tab stop), it will be pasted into a single cell in the Excel sheet.

▪ **Edit - Copy** or 📋 or ⌈Ctrl⌋ C

▪ Open the Excel application, if necessary, then the workbook in which you want to paste the copied data.

▪ Activate the first destination cell for the copy.

▪ **Edit - Paste** or 📋 or ⌈Ctrl⌋ V

Importing data by copying and establishing a link

When a link is established, any modifications to the data in the source file are carried over into the Microsoft Excel sheet.

▪ Open the application then the file in which the data you want to copy are stored.

▪ Select the data you want to copy.

▪ **Edit - Copy** or 📋 or ⌈Ctrl⌋ C

▪ Open the Excel application, if necessary then open the workbook where you wish to paste the data.

» Activate the first destination cell for the copied data.

» **Edit - Paste Special**

» Activate the **Paste link** option.

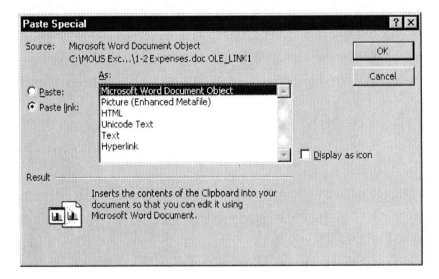

» Using the **As** list, select the format in which the data should be pasted.

» Activate the **Display as icon** option if you want the linked data to appear in the form of an icon.

» Click **OK**.

When opening an Excel workbook, you can choose to update the data.

Importing an object

An object is part or the whole of a document originating from another application.

» Open the workbook then activate the sheet in which you want to embed the object.

» **Insert - Object**

If you are embedding an existing file into the sheet, click the **Create from File** tab then enter the path and file name in the **File name** box or click the **Browse** button to select the file.

    ❊ If you want to insert a new object, click the **Create New** tab.

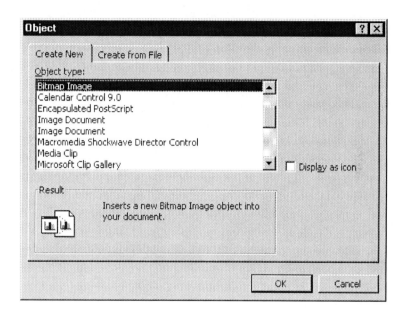

    ❊ In the **Object type** list, select the type of object you wish to embed into the worksheet.

    ❊ Click **OK**.

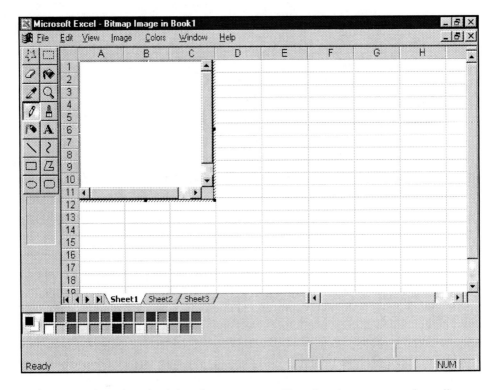

A frame with a hatched border appears. The Excel menus and toolbars are replaced by those of the application that will be used to create the object.

* Create the object using the tools and functions of the source (or server) application.

* When you have finished creating the object, click outside the object frame on the Excel worksheet to view the object in the sheet.

* To edit the object, double-click the embedded object.

* Save then close the workbook.

Importing an entire file

It is possible to import a file saved in an application other than Microsoft Excel (Lotus1-2-3, Quattro Pro, Microsoft Works, text file...).

※ **File - Open** or or Ctrl **O**

※ Open the **File of type** list then select the format of the file you want to import.

※ Select the file you want to import then click the **Open** button or double-click the file name.

※ If the file you are importing is a text file, follow the instructions in the **File Import Wizard** to define how the text should be distributed in the columns.

The imported file can now be seen on the screen in its original format. You must now save the file in Microsoft Excel format.

※ **File - Save** or ⊞ or Ctrl **S**

※ In the **Save as type** list, select the **Microsoft Excel Workbook (*.xls)** option.

※ If necessary, change the drive and/or folder where the workbook should be saved then change the **File Name**.

※ Click the **Save** button.

▪ Importing a table from an HTML file

To import a table from an HTML file to use it in Excel, you can create a Web query.

※ **Data - Get External Data - New Web Query**

※ In the first text box, enter the name of the Web page containing the table or click the **Browse Web** button to open your browser and look for the Web page.

※ Return to the **New Web Query** dialog box in the Excel application by clicking the corresponding button on the taskbar.

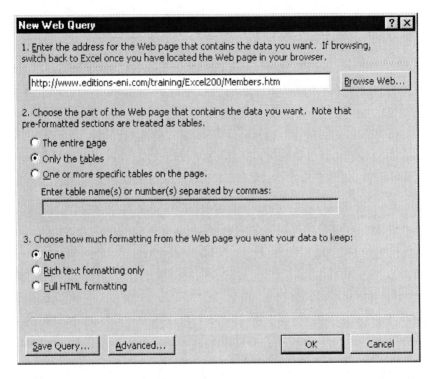

The address of the Web page found by the browser appears in the text box. Remember to close the browser window afterwards.

※ Activate one of the three options in step 2 to define which part of the Web page you want to import:

The entire page	Extracts the whole of the Web page (text, tables and other data).
Only the tables	Extracts all the tables and all the pre-formatted sections of the Web page.
One or more specific tables on the page	Extracts tables or pre-formatted sections from the Web page, when you enter the numbers or names of these elements.

*Pre-formatted sections (that already have a format applied) are parts of Web pages created in a format that allows you to use them in another application (Excel for example); click the **Advanced** button to see extra options concerning this type of section.*

▪ Activate one of the three options in step 3 to define the parts of the Web page's formatting that you wish to keep on your data:

None	Imports the data without any of the Web page formatting.
Rich text formatting only	Keeps only the formatting elements that Microsoft Excel is capable of reproducing. For example, hyperlinks and merged cells are not retained.
Full HTML formatting	Keeps all the Web page formatting including advanced formatting elements.

▪ If you want to be able to extract the query data into other workbooks or share the query with other users, click the **Save Query** button, change the **File name** if necessary then click the **Save** button.

*By default, the Web query is saved in an **.iqy** file, stored in the **C:\Windows\Application Data\Microsoft\Queries** folder.*

If you do not save the Web query in an .iqy folder, it will be saved as an item in your workbook and you will only be able to run it from that workbook.

▪ Click the **OK** button.

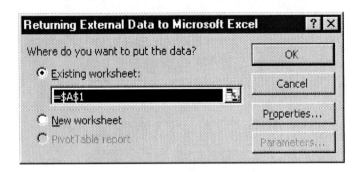

The **Returning External Data to Excel** dialog box appears, so you can choose where you want to insert the table in your workbook.

※ If you wish to insert the imported data into an **Existing worksheet**, activate the appropriate option then click the 🔜 button.
Go to the worksheet then click the first destination cell for the external data then click the 🔲 button to see the dialog box again.

To insert the table into a **New worksheet**, activate that option.

※ Click **OK**.

※ If Excel prompts you to do so, enter your **User name** and your **Password** then click **OK**.

The data from the imported table appear on the screen.

 To use a saved query, use the command **Data - Get External Data - Run Saved Query**, double-click the query you wish to run then activate the appropriate option, depending on where in the workbook you wish to insert the data. Click **OK**.

With this method, data from a table on a Web page is dragged onto an Excel workbook. This method does not, of course, create a Web query.

» Open your Web browser then enter the address of the Web page that contains the data you wish to import.

» If necessary, open the Excel application then the workbook concerned and activate the worksheet into which you want to import the Web page data.

The next step is to show both application windows on the screen simultaneously.

» RIGHT-click an empty space on the taskbar.

» Click the **Tile Windows Horizontally** or **Tile Windows Vertically** option, depending on how you want to arrange the windows on the screen.

» In your browser, select the data that you want to import into the Microsoft Excel sheet.

» Point to the selected data.

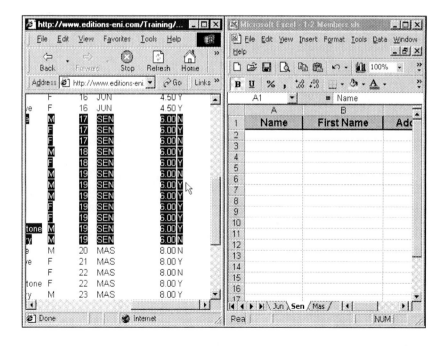

* Drag the selection to the Microsoft Excel application window, then onto the place in the worksheet where you wish to insert the imported data. When you are satisfied with the location, release the mouse button.

As you drag, the mouse pointer is accompanied by a plus sign within a rectangle; the imported data are copied into the Microsoft Excel worksheet.

▦4 ▪ Exporting data to other applications

Exporting data by dragging

With this method, data are dragged from a Microsoft Excel workbook towards another application (for example, Access, Word…).

* If necessary, open the Excel application then the workbook concerned and activate the sheet containing the data you wish to export.

* Open the application then the file into which you want to export the Excel data.

* Display both application windows on the screen at once by right-clicking an empty space on the taskbar and choosing the **Tile Windows Horizontally** or **Tile Windows Vertically** option depending on how you want to arrange your windows on the screen.

* On the Microsoft Excel worksheet, select the cells containing the data you wish to export.

* Point to one of the edges of the selected range.

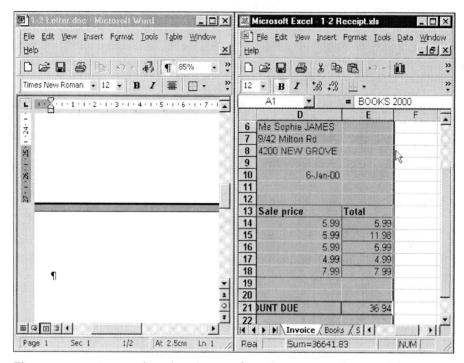

The mouse pointer takes the shape of a white arrow. Be careful not to point to the fill handle.

» Hold down the [Ctrl] key the drag the selected cells towards the destination application, to the position where you want the data to appear.

As you drag, the mouse pointer is accompanied by a plus sign within a rectangle. Holding down the [Ctrl] key while you drag ensures that a copy is made.

» Release the mouse button then the [Ctrl] key.

Exporting data by copying without establishing a link

* If necessary, open the Excel application then the workbook containing the data you wish to export.

* Select the cells containing the data to be exported.

* **Edit - Copy** or or ⌃Ctrl C

* Open the application then the file in which you wish to paste the data.

* Click the place where you want to paste the data.

* **Edit - Paste** or or ⌃Ctrl V

Exporting data by copying and establishing a link

When a link is in place, any changes made to the data in the original Microsoft Excel workbook are carried over into the file containing the exported data.

* Open the Excel application if necessary then open the workbook containing the data you want to copy.

* **Edit - Copy** or or ⌃Ctrl C

* Open the application and the file into which you want to paste the Excel data.

* Click the position where the data should be pasted.

* **Edit - Paste Special**

* Activate the **Paste link** option.

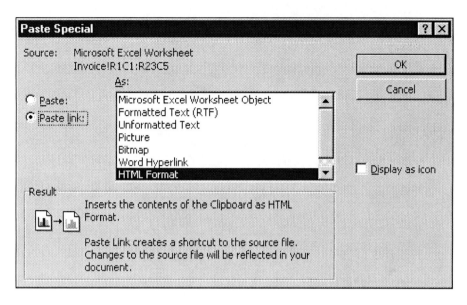

* From the **As** list, select the format in which you want to paste the data.

* Activate the **Display as icon** option if you want the linked data to be displayed in the form of an icon.

* Click **OK**.

Exporting an entire file

The aim of this technique is to open a Microsoft Excel file in another application. To do this, the other application must be able to manage Excel files.

* Open the application in which you want to open the Microsoft Excel workbook.

* **File - Open** or ⬚ or ⬚ **O**

* Open the **Files of type** list then select the **Microsoft Excel** format.

* Select the drive and folder in which the Excel workbook is stored.

* Select the file then click the **Open** button or double-click the file name.

※ If necessary, fill in any dialog boxes that appear subsequently; the contents of these dialog boxes change depending on the application you are using to open the Microsoft Excel workbook.

The Excel file can now be seen on the screen in its original format (.xls). You should save the file in the format of the application to which you are exporting it.

※ **File - Save As**

※ In the **Save as type** list, select the format of the active application.

※ If necessary, modify the drive or folder where the file will be saved then change the **File name**.

※ Click the **Save** button.

Inserting a workbook into another application as an object

※ Open the application then the file in which you want to insert a Microsoft Excel object.

※ **Insert - Object**

※ Activate the **Create from File** tab.

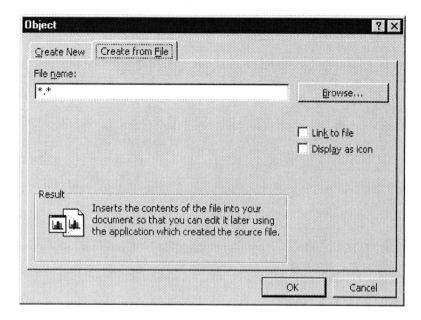

» Enter the path and name of the file you want to insert or click the **Browse** button to select it.

» Click **OK**.

» To edit the object, double-click the embedded object.

A frame with hatched borders appears. The Microsoft Excel menus and toolbars replace those of the active application.

» To view the object within the other application again, click outside the object's frame.

Below, you can see **Practice Exercise** 1.2. This exercise is made up of 4 steps. If you do not know how to complete one of the steps, go back to the lesson to refer to the corresponding title. When you have finished, check your work by reading the **Solution** on the next page.

All the steps in this exercise are likely to be tested in the exam.

☞ Practice Exercise 1.2

1. Import into a new Excel worksheet all the data contained in the **1-2 Client List.txt** document located in the **MOUS Excel 2000 Expert** folder. These data are **Delimited** and the delimiter is the **Tab**.

2. Import into **Sheet1** of the **1-2 Expenses Sheet.xls** workbook the data contained in the table of the **1-2 Expenses.doc** document. The data should be copied without a link and the first destination cell for the copied data is cell **A14**.
   Both **1-2 Expenses.doc** and **1-2 Expenses Sheet.xls** are located in the **MOUS Excel 2000 Expert** folder.

3. From the Web page located at this address: http://www.editions-eni.com/training/Excel2000/Members.htm, import the list of members that make up the **SEN** category into the **SEN** sheet in the **1-2 Members.xls** workbook.

4. Copy cells **A1** to **E23** from the **Receipt** sheet in the **1-2 Receipt.xls** workbook (in the **MOUS Excel 2000 Expert** folder), into the second page of the **1-2 Letter.doc** document (also in the **MOUS Excel 2000 Expert** folder). A link should be established when you make the copy.

If you want to put what you have learnt into practice on a real document, you can work on summary exercise 1 for the MANAGING DATA section, that you can find at the end of this book.

It is often possible to perform a task in several different ways, but here only the quickest solution is presented. Go back to the lesson to see the other techniques that can be used.

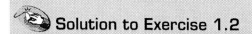

Solution to Exercise 1.2

1. To import into a new Excel worksheet all the data contained in the 1-2 Client List.txt text file, click the ⬜ tool to create a new workbook.

   Use the **Data - Get External Data** command then click the **Import Text File** option.
   Select the **MOUS Excel 2000 Expert** folder, click the **1-2 Client List.txt** file name then click the **Import** button.
   Under **Original data type**, make sure the **Delimited** option is active then click the **Next** button.

   Under **Delimiters,** leave the **Tab** option activated then click **Next**.
   Click **Finish**.
   Check that the **Existing worksheet** option is active, click, for example, cell **A3** in **Sheet1** then click **OK**.
   Save the workbook if you wish.

2. To import the data contained in the 1-2 Expenses.doc document into Sheet1 of the 1-2 Expenses Sheet.xls worksheet, open the Word application then open the **1-2 Expenses.doc** document contained in the **MOUS Excel 2000 Expert** folder.
   Click inside the table, use the **Table - Select - Table** command then click the 🔲 tool.

   If it is not open, open the Excel application then open the **1-2- Expenses Sheet.xls** workbook in the **MOUS Excel 2000 Expert** folder.

   Click cell **A14** on **Sheet1** then click the 🔲 tool.

Click the 🖫 tool to save the changes made.

🔲 3. To import the list of members belonging to the SEN category from the Web page http://www.editions-eni.com /training/Excel2000/Members.htm into the SEN sheet of the 1-2 Members.xls workbook, open the **1-2-Members.xls** workbook in the **MOUS Excel 2000 Expert** folder then click the **SEN** sheet tab.
Open your Web browser (internet Explorer for example), type **http://www.editions-eni.com/training/Excel2000/Members.htm** in the **Address** box then press the ⏎ key.

Scroll through the list to view until you can see the members in the **SEN** category.
Right click an empty space on the taskbar then click the **Tile Windows Vertically** option.
Position the pointer just before the **A** in Anderson (Terry), then drag down to the **N** in the Paid column of the row for O'Brian (Sean).
Point to the selection then drag it to cell **A2** on the **SEN** sheet in the Microsoft Excel application window.

Click the 🖫 tool to save the changes made in the **1-2 Members.xls** workbook then close your browser, if necessary.

🔲 4. To copy cells A1 to E23 of the Receipt sheet in the 1-2 Receipt.xls workbook into the second page of the 1-2 Letter.doc Word document, open the **1-2 Receipt.xls** workbook in the **MOUS Excel 2000 Expert** folder and activate the **Receipt** sheet tab.

Select cells **A1** to **E23** then click the 🗐 tool.
Open the Word application then the **1-2 Letter.doc** file in the **MOUS Excel 2000 Expert** folder and scroll down the document so you can click at the top of the second page.

Use the **Edit - Paste Special** command and activate the **Paste link** option.
In the **As** list, click the **Formatted Text (RTF)** option then click **OK**.

Click the 🖫 tool to save the changes made to the document.

MANAGING DATA
Lesson 1.3: Formatting

▥1 ▪ **Formatting numerical values**

🖰 ▪ Select the values concerned by the formatting.

▪ Choose one of the formats below:

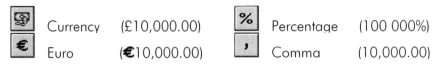

🔲	Currency	(£10,000.00)	%	Percentage (100 000%)
€	Euro	(€10,000.00)	,	Comma (10,000.00)

📄 ▪ Select the values concerned.

▪ **Format - Cell**

▪ Click the **Number** tab.

▪ In the **Category** list, select the category of the format you want to use.

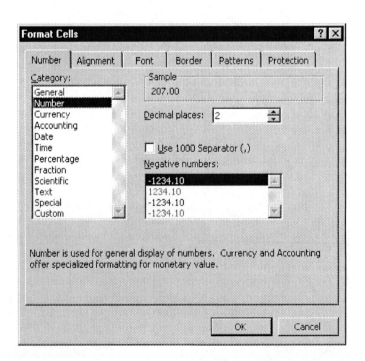

- If necessary, modify the format settings; for example, you can specify the number of decimal places.

- Click **OK**.

> 📄 *Hash symbols may appear in some cells if the column is not wide enough to display the selected format.*

> 🖱 *To display one more or one less decimal place, select the cells concerned and use the ⊞ tool or the ⊞ tool.*

2 ▪ Creating a custom number format

- Select the cells concerned by the formatting.

- **Format - Cell** or ⌨ **1**

  If you choose to use the shortcut key, use the 1 on the alphanumeric keyboard.

- If necessary, activate the **Number** tab.

- Select the **Custom** format from the **Category** list.

- In the **Type** list, choose the format that is closest to the one you want.

  The #,##0 code indicates that a comma should be inserted between thousands and hundreds.

▪ Enter your custom format in the **Type** box:

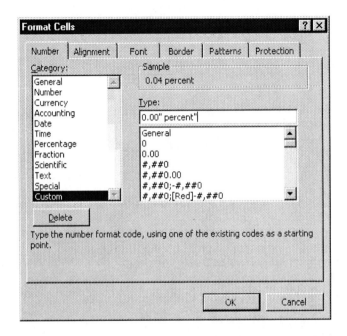

Any text that has been included in the format must be entered between inverted commas. Be very careful with the spaces you enter: if you enter a space outside of the inverted commas, Excel interprets it as a request to divide by a thousand.

▪ Click **OK**.

3 ▪ Creating conditional formats

You can, for example, choose to display in red only those cells that contain a number less than 1000.

▪ Select the cells concerned by the format.

▪ **Format - Conditional Formatting**

* In the **Condition 1** drop-down list select:

Cell Value Is   if the condition concerns the value contained in the cells (constant or the result of a formula).

Formula Is   if the condition concerns a logical formula.

* In the first case, the next thing to do is select a comparison operator then a comparison value. In the second case, define the logical formula (the result of this type of formula is TRUE or FALSE).
  If the condition concerns a formula, start it with an equals sign (=).

* Click the **Format** button.

* Use the options in the **Font**, **Border** and **Patterns** tabs to define the format that is to be applied to the cells when the condition is fulfilled.

* Click **OK**.

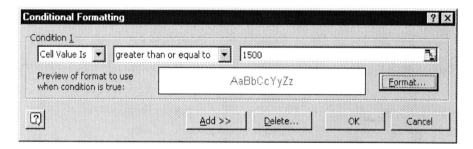

* To define other formats to be applied under different conditions (particularly to define a format to be used when the preceding condition is not fulfilled), click the **Add>>** button then define another conditional format in the same way.

* Click **OK**.

The cell format changes automatically according to the contents of the cell

Below, you can see **Practice Exercise** 1.3. This exercise is made up of 3 steps. If you do not know how to complete one of the steps, go back to the lesson to refer to the corresponding title. When you have finished, check your work by reading the **Solution** on the next page.

All the steps in this exercise are likely to be tested in the exam.

👉 Practice Exercise 1.3

In order to complete exercise 1.3 you should open *1-3 Furniture.xls* in the *MOUS Excel 2000 Expert* folder and activate *Sheet1*.

1. Apply a **Comma** format to cells **B5** to **D19** and to cells **F5** to **F19** then remove the decimal places.

2. Create a custom number format for cells **G5** to **G20** that will display the values, followed by a space then the word **percent** (for example: 11.96 percent).

3. Create conditional formats that will show profits (F5 to F19) greater than or equal to 1500 in red and the others in blue.

If you want to put what you have learned into practice in a real document, you can work on summary exercise 1 for the MANAGING DATA section that you can find at the end of this book.

It is often possible to perform a task in several different ways, but here only the quickest solution is presented. Go back to the lesson to see the other techniques that can be used.

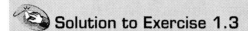

Solution to Exercise 1.3

1. To apply the comma format to cells B5 to D19 and cells F5 to F19, select cells **B5** to **D19** and **F5** to **F19** then click the [,] tool.

    To remove the decimal places, keep cells B5 to D19 and F5 to F19 selected and click the [.00/.0] tool twice.

2. To create a custom number format for cells G5 to G20 that displays the values, leaves a space, then the word "percent" (for example 11.96 percent), select cells **G5** to **G20**, run **Format - Cells** then click the **Number** tab.
    Select the **Custom** format in the **Category** list, then click the **0.00** option in the **Type** list.
    Click after **0.00** in the **Type** text box and type "[Space] percent".
    Click **OK** to confirm.

MANAGING DATA
Exercise 1.3: Formatting

3. To create conditional formats that will show profits made (F5 to F19) that are greater than or equal to 1500 in red and the others in blue, select cells **F5** to **F19** then use **Format - Conditional Formatting**.
Leave the **Cell Value Is** selected, select the **greater than or equal to** comparison operator in the second list and enter **1500** in the following text box.
Click the **Format** button then the **Font** tab. Select the colour red in the **Color** list and click **OK**.

Click the **Add>>** button to define the second format that is to be applied (condition 2). Leave the **Cell Value Is** option selected and select the **less than** comparison operator in the second list then enter **1500** in the following text box.
Click the **Format** button then the **Font** tab and select the colour blue in the **Color** list then click **OK**. Click **OK**.

MANAGING DATA
Lesson 1.4: Outlines

1 • Creating an outline

An outline allows you to see or print only the main results of a table without the detail of the data.

Creating an outline automatically

» Click in the table concerned.

» **Data - Group and Outline - Auto Outline**

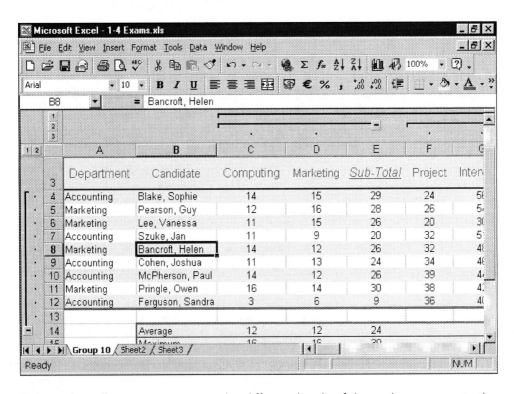

Buttons that allow you to manage the different levels of the outline appear to the left and at the top of the worksheet.

Creating an outline manually

» Select the rows (or columns) that are to be hidden.

» **Data - Group and Outline - Group**.

» To insert a column (or a row) in the group with the preceding level, select the column (or row) then use **Data - Group and Outline - Group**.

» To remove a column (or a row) from a group, select the column (or row) and use **Data - Group and Outline - Ungroup**.

» Use the ⊟ and ⊞ buttons to collapse or expand the outline.

⊞2 ▪ Using outlines

» To hide lower-level columns or rows, click the corresponding ⊟ button.

» To hide all the groups in the same level, click the numbered button that corresponds to the level.

	A	B	E	H	I	J
3	Department	Candidate	_Sub-Total_	_Sub-Total_	_Overall Total_	
4	Accounting	Blake, Sophie	29	80	109	
5	Marketing	Pearson, Guy	28	80	108	
6	Marketing	Lee, Vanessa	26	50	76	
7	Accounting	Szuke, Jan	20	83	103	
8	Marketing	Bancroft, Helen	26	80	106	
9	Accounting	Cohen, Joshua	24	80	104	
10	Accounting	McPherson, Paul	26	83	109	
11	Marketing	Pringle, Owen	30	80	110	
12	Accounting	Ferguson, Sandra	9	76	85	
13						
14		Average	24			
15		Maximum	30			

In the screen above, the level 2 columns are no longer visible. The ⊟ _buttons have become_ ⊞.

* To redisplay the lower-level columns or rows, click each ⊞ button, or click the button that corresponds to the next level (for example, click button **3** to redisplay all the level **2** groups).

3 ▪ Clearing an outline

* Click in the table concerned.

* **Data - Group and Outline - Clear Outline**

⊞4 ▪ Inserting rows of statistics

This action allows you to insert sub-total rows that will calculate a sum, an average...

▪ Sort the table by the column that contains the entries you want to group together, as a first step to producing a subtotal for each group. For example: to display the average for each department, the table should be sorted according to the contents of the Department column.

▪ Click in the table concerned by the statistics rows.

▪ **Data - Subtotals**

▪ In the **At each change in** list, select the column that contains the groups that are to be used for the statistical calculation.

▪ Choose the calculation to be made in the **Use function** list.

▪ Tick the columns that contain the values that you want to use in the calculation.

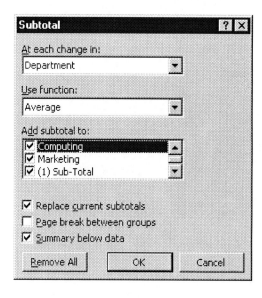

- Leave the **Replace current subtotals** option active if you want to replace any existing subtotals with those that you are creating.

- Activate the **Page break between groups** option to automatically insert a page break after each group of subtotals.

- Leave the **Summary below data** option active if you want to create subtotals and totals beneath detailed data. If this option is deactivated, only the subtotals will appear below the detailed data.

- Click **OK**.

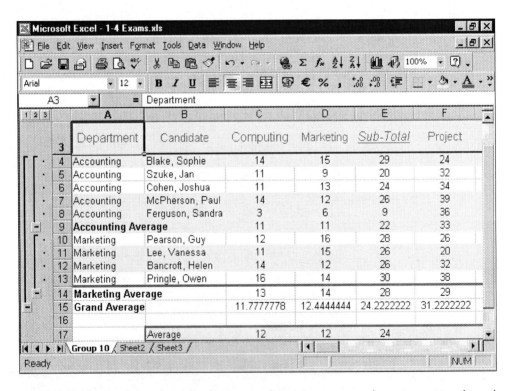

Excel calculates the subtotals that provide statistics you have requested and creates an outline that allows you to show or hide the detail rows that correspond to each subtotal.

Below, you can see **Practice Exercise** 1.4. This exercise is made up of 4 steps. If you do not know how to complete one of the steps, go back to the lesson to refer to the corresponding title. When you have finished, check your work by reading the **Solution** on the next page.

All the steps in this exercise are likely to be tested in the exam.

Practice Exercise 1.4

*In order to complete exercise 1.4 you should open **1-4 Exams.xls** in the MOUS Excel 2000 Expert folder.*

1. Create an Auto Outline of the cell range **A3** (**Department**) to **I12** (**85**); now remove columns **F** (**Project**) and **G** (**Interview**) from the outline.

2. Collapse the outline using the ⊟ button so that the **Computing** and **Marketing** columns are hidden, then use the numbered button to display only the first level.

3. Clear the whole outline.

4. Insert rows of statistics for all of the columns in the table, using the **Average** function.

If you want to put what you have learned into practice in a real document, you can work on summary exercise 1 for the MANAGING DATA section that you can find at the end of this book.

It is often possible to perform a task in several different ways, but here only the quickest solution is presented. Go back to the lesson to see the other techniques that can be used.

 Solution to Exercise 1.4

1. To create an auto outline for cells A3 to I12, select this cell range then use **Data - Group and Outline - Auto Outline**.

   To remove columns **F** and **G** from the outline, select them by dragging over their column-headers, then use **Data - Group and Outline - Ungroup**.

2. To hide the **Computing** and **Marketing** columns, click the ⊟ button above column **E**.

   To show only the first level of the outline, click the 🔢 numbered button in the top left corner of the worksheet.

3. To clear the whole plan, click one of the cells in the table, then use **Data - Group and Outline - Clear Outline**.

4. Before inserting **Average** statistic rows, sort the data in the table using the ⬇ tool after having clicked in a cell in the **Department** column (**A3 to A12**).

   Once the data have been sorted, stay in the table and use **Data - Subtotals**.
   In the **Use function** drop-down list, choose the **Average** function.
   In the **Add subtotal to** list, tick the options for which a calculation is to be made, in this case: **Computing**, **Marketing**, **(1) Sub-total**, **Project**, **Interview**, **(2) Sub-total**, then click **OK**.

MANAGING DATA
Lesson 1.5: Lists of data

MANAGING DATA
Lesson 1.5: Lists of data

1 ▪ Using the data form

What is a list of data?

A list of data is commonly called a database.

▪ Each separate column of data constitutes a FIELD.

	A	B	C	D	E	F
1	**Name**	**First Name**	**Address**	**PC/City**	**Sex**	**Age**
2	Alderman	Christine	56 Harvey St	4100 Tewesbury	F	13
3	Andrews	Melissa	27 Ridley St	5600 St Lucia	F	15
4	Barnett	Frances	38 Harrison Cres	4500 Greerton	F	15
5	Charles	Yolanda	29 Bartlett Cres	6000 Lorton	F	14
6	Cray	Hannah	77 Kennedy Drive	5800 Rafter	F	17
7	Dell	Tammy	13 Read Road	4300 Dryden	F	16
8	Dorcas	Michelle	10 Kings Ct	5400 Fern Grove	F	16
9	Grant	Jessica	14/196 Red Sand Road	6100 Herston	F	17
10	Grey	Josephine	89 Green St	5500 Killybill	F	22
11	Greene	Louise	45 West Road	5600 St Lucia	F	25
12	Hunt	Rosemary	32 Fern Drive	5000 Gunston	F	18

On the example above, you have 6 fields, which correspond to the column headings - Name, First Name, Address, PC/City, Sex, Age.

▪ Each field must have a column heading, which becomes its <u>name</u>. There are no restrictions on the name you can give but short, clear field names are easier to manage.

▪ The first row of the database contains the field names and all the other rows are **RECORDS**.

The data form is used to enter records but can also be used to search for a particular record.

Accessing the form

» Click a cell in the table that you want to manage as a database. This table should contain the field names and at least one record:

	A	B	C	D	E	F
1	**Name**	**First Name**	**Address**	**PC/City**	**Sex**	**Age**
35	Kelsey	Ross	12/15 Sth Canal Way	4300 Dryden	M	27
36	Layton	Campbell	16 Jules Road	4100 Tewesbury	M	23
37	Lincoln	James	"One Tree", Devlin Ct	5300 Emerald Bay	M	25

» **Data - Form**

This form is made up of the following elements:

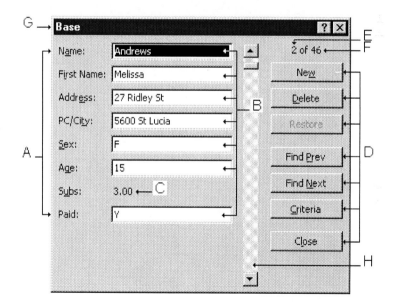

A   Field names

B   Edit boxes for entering field contents

C   Data form fields containing computed fields

D   Command buttons

E   The number of the current record

F   The total number of records

G   Title bar

H   Vertical scroll bar

Adding records

▫ To start adding a new record, click the **New** button.

▫ Fill in each new record as follows:

- press `Tab` to move to the next box, except after the last one (or `Shift` `Tab` if you want to go back to the previous box).

- to confirm the data entered, press ⏎ after the last piece of information is entered; you will go immediately into a new record.

Moving from record to record

▫ Use the scroll bar or the arrow keys, as shown below:

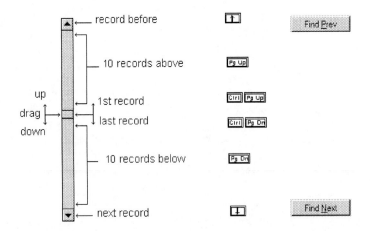

The last form displayed is always a new form ready to be filled in.

Finding to a particular record

» Go into either the first or last record.

» Click the **Criteria** button.

*The record number indicator is replaced by the word **Criteria**, the calculated fields become text boxes and the **Criteria** button is replaced by a **Form** button.*

» Set your search conditions as if you were filling in a record but do not press ↵. For example:

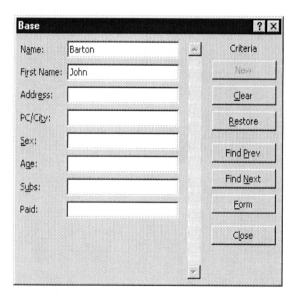

These criteria should return any records listed under the name of John Barton.

» If you started from the first record, click the **Find Next** button to begin searching. If you started at the last record, start searching with the **Find Prev** button.

» Continue your search using the **Find Next** or **Find Prev** buttons.

Modifying a record

▪ Go to the record you want to modify.

▪ Make your corrections then press ⏎ to confirm them.

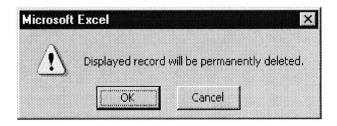 *If you change your mind about the changes you make, click the* **Restore** *button (before pressing ⏎) to go back to the previous values.*

Deleting a record

▪ Go to the record you want to delete.

▪ Click the **Delete** button.

Microsoft Excel	☒
⚠ Displayed record will be permanently deleted.	
OK	Cancel

▪ Confirm the deletion with **OK**.

Leaving the data form

▪ Click the **Close** button.

▥2 ▪ Creating and using a simple filter

A filter is used to select records that correspond to a set criterion.

Activating AutoFilter

▪ Activate one of the cells in the list of data.

▪ **Data - Filter - AutoFilter**

Each field becomes a drop-down list that can be opened by clicking the down arrow to the right of the field name.

Filtering by one of the values listed

▪ Open the list associated with the field concerned.

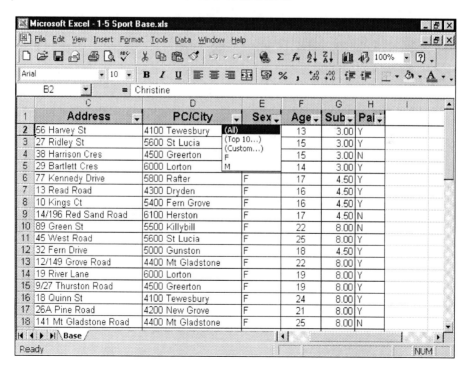

Each list includes all the values in the field.

- Click the value that interests you.

  All the records that do not concern the selected value are hidden automatically. On the status bar, Excel indicates the number of records that meet your criterion and the row numbers of the records displayed change colour.

Filtering by a specific criterion

- Open the list associated with the field concerned.
- Click **Custom**.
- In the first list box, select an operator of comparison.
- Activate the text box next to it and enter the compare value.

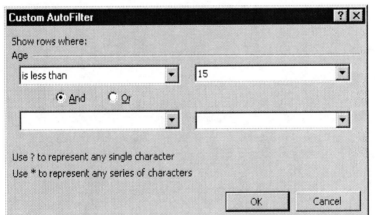

This criterion filters all the records for people aged under 15.

- Click **OK**.

Filtering the highest and lowest values

- Open the list associated with the field concerned.
- Click **(Top 10...)**.

▫ Indicate whether you want to see the **Top** values or the **Bottom** values.

▫ Specify how many of the top/bottom values you want to see.

▫ Choose **Items** to filter all the records corresponding to the criteria (top or bottom) or **Percent** to filter a number of rows corresponding to a percentage of the total number of values in the list.

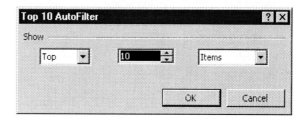

▫ Click **OK**.

▥ 3 ▪ Filtering by several criteria

Two criteria for the same field

▫ Activate the **AutoFilter**.

▫ Open the list for the field concerned.

▫ Click **Custom**.

▫ Define the first filter criterion.

▫ Indicate how the two criteria are to be combined:

  - if both must be satisfied together, choose **And**,

  - if either one or the other must be satisfied, choose **Or**.

▫ Enter your second condition.

▫ Click **OK**.

Criteria concerning several fields, combined with "and"

* Activate **AutoFilter**.

* Set the conditions in each field concerned.

▩4 ▪ Creating a complex filter

Creating a criteria range

* You first need to locate an empty space of a few columns and a few rows on the sheet (typically next to the list of data).

* In one of the empty rows, enter the field names you want to use to filter the list.

* In the rows below, enter the criteria that should be met, paying attention to the following rules:

Combination	Method
OR	the criteria are entered in several rows
AND	the criteria are entered in several columns
OR and AND	the criteria are entered in several rows and several columns

Look at these examples to better understand the use of AND and OR when setting criteria:

Requirements	Criteria ranges	
Records for members named: BARNETT **OR** SANDERS **OR** KELSEY	NAME	
	BARNETT	
	SANDERS	
	KELSEY	
Records for 18 year-old girls: 18 **AND** F	AGE	SEX
	18	F
Records for boys aged 13 **OR** 15 **OR** 17 years	SEX	AGE
	M	13
	M	15
	M	17

Using a criteria range

» Click the data list.

» **Data - Filter - Advanced Filter**

*The **Filter the list, in-place** option is active by default.*

» Click the **Criteria range** box, use the 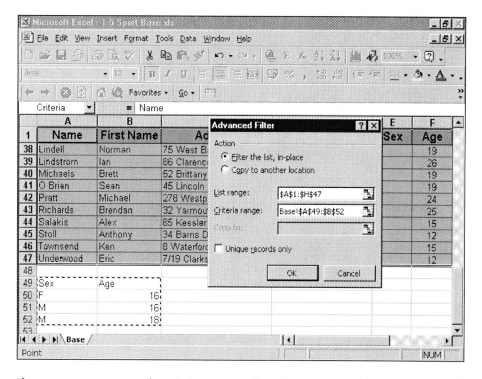 to collapse the dialog box and select the criteria range previously created on the worksheet. Click ▦ to restore the dialog box:

» If necessary, activate the **Unique records only** option to filter out any duplicate records.

» Click **OK**.

📄   *The cells in the criteria range are now called **Criteria**.*

▣5 ▪ Showing all the records again

▪ If only one filter is active, open the drop-down list on the field that is filtered and click the **All** option.

▪ If several filters are active, use the **Data - Filter - Show All** command.

▣6 ▪ Copying records that meet filter criteria

▪ In another place on the sheet, enter a row of the field headings whose contents you wish to filter and extract.

▪ Create a criteria range.

▪ **Data - Filter - Advanced Filter**

▪ In the **Action** frame, activate the **Copy to another location** option.

*The **Copy to** box becomes available.*

▪ If necessary, indicate the location of the criteria range in **Criteria range**.

▪ Activate the **Copy to** box and select the row of names you have just typed in the sheet.

▪ Click **OK**.

📄   *If you change the criteria range, run the filter again.*

7 ▪ Sorting the data in a table

By a single criterion

▪ Select the table you want to sort.

▪ Use `Tab` or `Shift` `Tab` to activate a cell in the column by which you want to sort the table.

▪ Use:

to sort in ascending order.

to sort in descending order.

Holding down the `Shift` key and clicking produces the same effect as clicking.

By several criteria

▪ Select the table you wish to sort.

▪ **Data - Sort**

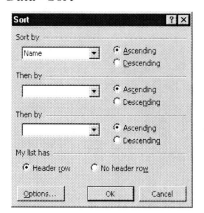

The table can be sorted by three different columns.

- In the data list, select the names of the fields that correspond to the columns by which you want to sort the table.

- For each column, specify whether to sort in **Ascending** or **Descending** order.

- Activate the **Header row** option if necessary to exclude the first row of the table from sorting.

- Click **OK**.

8 ▪ Defining authorised data for specific cells

- Select the cells concerned.

- **Data - Validation - Settings** tab

- Open the **Allow** list and choose an option appropriate to the type of data you wish to allow in the cell(s):

Any value	No restrictions.
Whole number	The cell must contain an integer.
Decimal	The cell must contain a number or a fraction.
List	This option allows you to list cell references containing authorised data.
Date	The cell must contain a date.
Time	The cell must contain a time.
Text length	This option allows you to specify the number of characters authorised in the cell.
Custom	This option allows you to enter a formula to limit the data that the cell will accept.

- If you select **Whole number**, **Decimal**, **Date**, or **Time**, choose an operator of comparison from the **Data** list and give values for comparison.

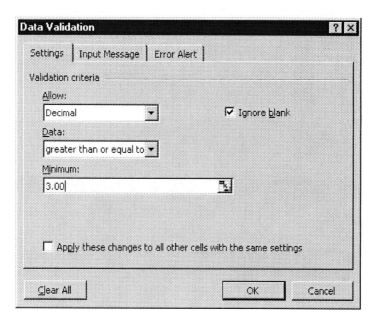

These validation criteria do not allow you to enter any data apart from numbers (decimals included) a value of 3.00 or more.

※ If you choose **List**, enter the references of the cells containing authorised data in the **Source** box. Activate the **In-cell dropdown** option if you want to add a drop-down list of authorised data to the cell(s) concerned.

※ If you select **Custom**, use the **Formula** box to enter a calculation formula beginning with an equal sign (=). This should be a logical type formula, that returns **TRUE** or **FALSE**.

※ Whatever the type of data specified, activate **Ignore blank** if you authorise the cell to remain empty.

※ Click the **Error Alert** tab to enter a message to display when the data entered do not meet the validation criteria.

※ Leave the **Show error alert after invalid data is entered** option active and set the following options:

Style	The symbol that will appear in the dialog box containing the error message.
Title	The title of the dialog box.
Error message	The text of the message.

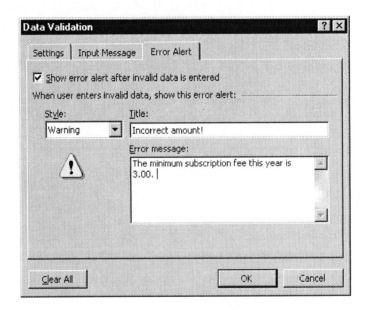

※ Click **OK**.

Any entry that does not correspond to the validation criteria will cause an error message to appear:

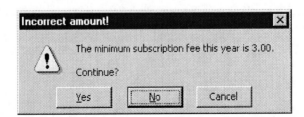

Any data entered previously are not checked: however, you can highlight any cells whose contents do not meet the validation criteria (see below).

*The options on the **Input Message** page of the **Data Validation** dialog box let you define a title and a message for a ScreenTip that will display when the pointer is on that cell.*

9 ▪ Tracing unauthorised data

This is a technique to find cells containing data that do not meet the validation criteria; any cells found will be circled in red:

1	Name	First Name	PC/City	Sex	Age	Subs	Paid
17	Peak	Alison	4200 New Grove	F	21	8.00	Y
18	Peyton	Theresa	4400 Mt Gladstone	F	25	8.00	N
19	Rowe	Patricia	4400 Mt Gladstone	F	15	3.00	N
20	Sanders	Heather	6100 Herston	F	12	2.50	N
21	Sm			F	12	2.50	N
22	Sta			F	15	3.00	Y
23	Sto			F	12	3.00	Y
24	Stoner	Carla	4000 Westport	F	15	3.00	N
25	Youmad	Alanna	5400 Fern Grove	F	13	2.50	Y
26	Anderson	Terry	5200 Abbeyville	M	17	4.50	N
27	Barton	John	4000 Westport	M	16	4.50	Y

Any subscriptions that are not equal to or greater than 3.00 are circled.

▪ Display the **Auditing** toolbar:
Tools - Auditing - Show Auditing Toolbar

▪ Click the ⊞ tool then click the worksheet.

▪ To remove the red circles, click ▥.

10 ▪ **Using Microsoft QUERY to import external data**

*It is possible to import data from a **relational** database such as Microsoft Access 2000 or from an **OLAP** database, such as Microsoft SQL Server OLAP, or from a **text file.** You can import this information directly into an Excel worksheet by using the Microsoft Query application.*

The principle of Microsoft Query is to create a query that will copy data from an external database into an Excel workbook and simultaneously sort and filter the imported data. One advantage of this technique is that you can exclude data that you do not require.

Microsoft Query is a Microsoft Excel option, which by default is only installed on your computer the first time you try to extract external data with Excel.

*During this lesson, you will see the import procedure for an (existing) ACCESS 2000 database, which is a **relational** database.*

Importing data

▪ Click the cell where you wish to begin inserting the external data.

This location can be modified once the import procedure is complete.

▪ **Data - Get External Data - New Database Query**

If the Microsoft Query application is not installed on your computer, Excel will prompt you to install it; if this occurs, follow the instructions provided to install it.

*The **Choose Data Source** dialog box appears.*

▪ If necessary, activate the **Databases** tab.

▪ In the list, select **MS Access Database** as the source of the data you wish to extract.

▪ Make sure the **Use the Query Wizard to create/edit queries** option is active.

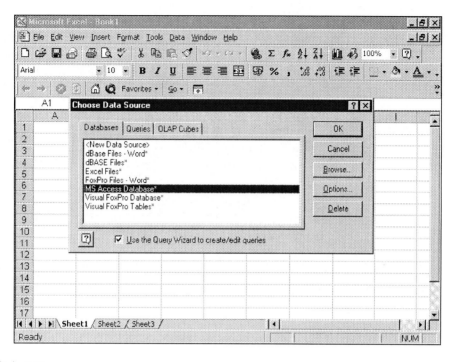

- Click **OK**.

- In the **Drives** list, choose the disk drive where the database is stored then in **Directories** choose its folder.

- Click to select the database that contains the information you want to extract then click **OK**.

  *The **Query Wizard** dialog box appears on the screen. The first step is to choose the columns (fields) to include in the query.*

- To see all the columns (fields) in a table, click the plus (+) sign you can see to the left of the table name, in the **Available tables and columns** list.

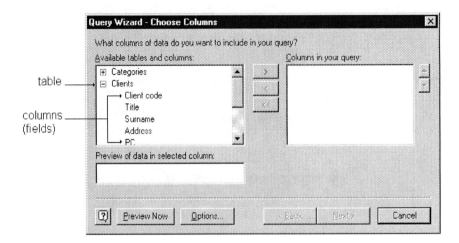

- For each complete table or column you want to add to the **Columns in your query** list, click the element to be added in the **Available tables and columns** list then click the [>] button.

If you add columns from different tables, Excel must be able to join those tables which means that at least one column, or field, in one table has a matching column or field in the other table. If this type of relationship does not exist between the two tables, you will be prompted to create one manually:

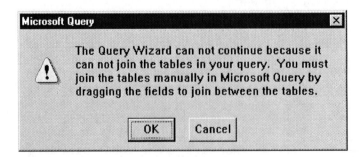

- Click **Next**.

*The **Filter Data** dialog box allows you to set filter criteria per column (field) in order to limit which data is imported. If no criteria are present, all the data in the column concerned will be imported.*

* For each column to be filtered:

  - Select in the **Column to filter** list the name of the column to which the filter should be applied.

  - Select the operator of comparison and the compare value in the **Include only rows where** boxes.

  *To delete a criterion, open the list of operators for the criterion concerned then click the empty space above the **equals** operator.*

* Activate the **And** or **Or** options to define one or more further filter criteria based on the same column: when the **And** option is active, all of the conditions set must be met simultaneously, and when the **Or** option is active, only one condition needs to be met.

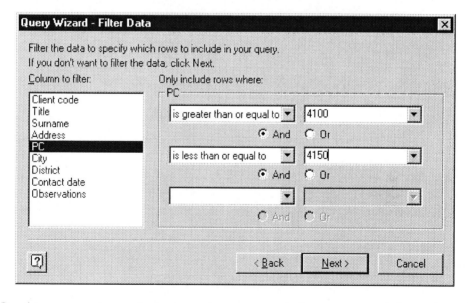

On this screen, two criteria have been entered, but you can define others if required.

- Click **Next**.

  *The **Sort Order** dialog box appears so you can sort the data as it is imported, if you wish.*

- Open the **Sort by** list and click the name of the column by which you want to sort the table, then choose whether you wish to sort in **Ascending** (from A to Z) or **Descending** (from Z to A) order.

- If the first column contains duplicate values, you can make a secondary sort by selecting another column in the **Then by** list and choosing an **Ascending** or **Descending** sort order.

- If necessary, repeat this operation for each of the columns you wish to use to sort the list.

  To delete a sort order, open the list box for the column concerned then click the empty space located above the name of the first column listed.

- Click **Next**.

- Make sure the **Return Data to Microsoft Excel** option is active in the **Finish** dialog box.

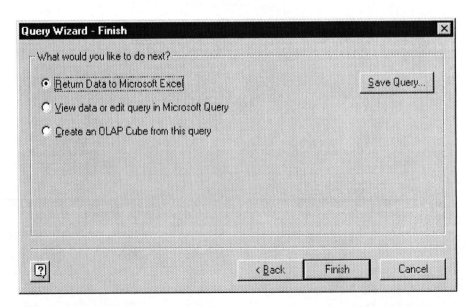

※ If you want to save your query and use it at a later date, click the **Save Query** button, give your query a **File name** then click the **Save** button.

By default, a Query file carries a .dqy extension and is saved in the c:/Windows/Application Data/Microsoft/Queries folder.

※ Click the **Finish** button to close the application and retrieve the data in Microsoft Excel.

*The **Returning External Data to Microsoft Excel** dialog box appears; you can choose where on the worksheet you want the data to be placed.*

※ To insert the data in an **Existing worksheet**, activate this option. The text box on this option contains the reference of the cell that was active when the import procedure first started. If you want to modify the active cell, click the 🔲 button to collapse the dialog box (if necessary) and click the first destination cell for the external data. Restore the dialog box by clicking 🔲.

※ To insert the data in a **New worksheet**, activate the corresponding option.

※ To manage the contains data from the query in a **PivotTable report**, activate that option.

※ Click **OK**.

*If you are importing to a new worksheet or an existing one, you can see the results of the query on the screen, along with the **External Data** toolbar. If this toolbar does not appear, you can open it yourself with the **View - Toolbars - External Data** command.*

Looking at the External Data toolbar

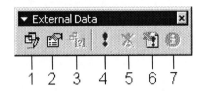

1. Is for editing the query by opening the Query application again so you can modify, if required, the list of columns to import or the filter and/or sort criteria in the query.

2. Displays the properties of the external data range so that you can edit then if necessary.

3. Used to specify the options for a special type of query.

4. Updates (refreshes) the external data by referring to changes made in the source data.

5. Cancels the previous update.

6. Updates (refreshes) the range of external data according to the source data and also updates any pivot tables or pivot charts linked to it.

7. Shows the **External Data Refresh Status** dialog box so you can see how the current update is evolving.

Updating ranges of external data

* Changes in the source of a range of external data can be carried over into the range on your sheet in one of several ways:

  - occasionally, by clicking the tool on the **External Data** toolbar, or,

  - automatically, by clicking the tool and defining the options in the **Refresh control** frame.

Below you can see **Practice Exercise** 1.5. This exercise is made up of 10 steps. If you do not know how to complete one of the steps, go back to the lesson to refer to the corresponding title. When you have finished, check your work by reading the **Solution** on the next page.

All the steps in this exercise are likely to be tested in the exam.

☞ Practice Exercise 1.5

*In order to complete Practice Exercise 1.5, you should open the **1-5 Sport Base** workbook in the **MOUS Excel 2000 Expert** folder.*

1. Using the data form, look for the record for club member called **John BARTON** and correct his address, which should read **27 Chambers St** instead of **37 Chambers St**.

2. Using a custom AutoFilter, find all the records in the list for members aged under **15** years.

3. Using an AutoFilter with several criteria, show all the members who have paid a subscription fee (sub) of **4.50**.

4. Show a list of the **girls** aged **16** as well as the **boys** aged between **16 AND 18** by using an advanced filter.

5. In one action, delete all the filter criteria and show all the records in the list again.

6. Copy the records extracted with the filter used in step 4(records for **girls** aged **16** and **boys** aged **16** and **18**), and insert them starting from cell **L8**. Only the **Surname, First Name** and **Address** fields corresponding to the filter should be copied.

7. Sort the data list in ascending order by the **Age** field.

8. Set a validation condition to the subscription fee cells, because the latest subscription fees should all exceed **3.00**.

9. Any values in the subscription column that do not meet the validation criteria should be circled in red (these should be any values below 3.00).

10. Using the Microsoft Query application, import the **Clients** table into the **1-5 Sport Base.xls** workbook. This table is located in the Access database called **Access database.mdb** that you can find in the **MOUS Excel 2000 Expert** folder.

If you want to put what you have learnt into practice on a real document, you can work on summary exercise 1 for the MANAGING DATA section, that you can find at the end of this book.

It is often possible to perform a task in several different ways, but here only the quickest solution is presented. Go back to the lesson to see the other techniques that can be used.

 Solution to Exercise 1.5

1. To display the data form, activate one of the cells in the list of data then use the **Data - Form** command.
To look for the record concerning **John Barton**, go to the first record in the list (use the vertical scroll bar if necessary) then click the **Criteria** button.
Click the text box for the **Name** field, in which you want to search and enter the name you are looking for: **Barton**. Use the ⎆ key to go to the text box for the **First Name** field and enter **John**.
Click the **Next** button to start searching.
To modify the contents of the **Address** field, click the corresponding text box then edit the street number, changing it from **37** to **27** and confirm by clicking the **Close** button.

2. To make a custom AutoFilter, activate one of the cells in the list then use the **Data - Filter - AutoFilter** command.
Open the list associated with the **Age** field then click the **Custom** option.

MANAGING DATA
Exercise 1.5: Lists of data

Fill in the dialog box, following the example below:

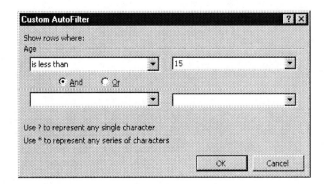

Then confirm by clicking **OK**.

3. To make an AutoFilter with several criteria on the data list, the **AutoFilter** command in **Data - Filter** must be active.
   Open the list associated with the **SUBS** column (Subscription fee) and click the required value: **4.50**, which corresponds to the first criterion; then open the second list on the **Paid** field and click **Y** (for Yes) which is the second criterion.

4. To show a list of all the girl club members aged 16 and all the boys aged 16 and 18,you should determine the fields and values on which the filters will be run, so your criteria range will resemble the example below:

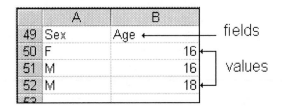

Click any cell in the data list then run an advanced filter with the **Data - Filter - Advanced Filter** command.

Activate the **Filter the list, in-place** option and fill in the **List range** and **Criteria range** boxes.

5. To show all the records again, deleting all the filter criteria, use the **Data - Filter - Show All** command.

6. To copy the records returned by the filter set up in step 4, use the criteria range you created previously and enter the field names that you want copying, as shown below:

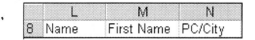

Run the advanced filter by using the **Data - Filter - Advanced Filter** command. Activate the **Copy to another location** option, check the **List range** and **Criteria range** boxes and fill in the **Copy to** box.

7. To sort the list of data, start by selecting all the records, from **A1** to **H47**, then use the **Data - Sort** command.
Open the list on the **Sort by** box and click **Age**. Ensure the **Ascending** option is active then click the **Header row** option.
Confirm your sort order with **OK**.

8. To set validation criteria in the subscription fee cells, start by selecting all the cells in the **Subs** column and use **Data - Validation - Settings** tab.
Open the **Allow** list and choose the **Whole number** option. In the **Data** list, choose **greater than or equal to** as the operator. In the **Minimum** box, enter a value of **3.00**. Confirm your entry by clicking **OK**.

9. To trace the values in the Subs column that do not meet the validation criteria (values less than 3.00), show the **Auditing** toolbar with the **Tools - Auditing - Show Auditing Toolbar** command. Click the ⊞ tool then, if necessary, use the vertical scroll bar to locate the cells circled in red.

10. To import external data (from a relational database) through the Microsoft Query application, start by activating an empty cell in the **1-5 Sport Base.xls** workbook (for example, cell **A54**).
Use the **Data - External Data - New Database Query** command.
In the **Choose Data Source** dialog box, activate the **Database** tab then select the source as **MS Access Database** in the list offered.
Make sure that the **Use Query Wizard to create/edit queries** option is active before clicking **OK**.

In the **Select Database** dialog box, use the **Directories** list to select the **Access database.mdb** database from the **MOUS Excel 2000 Expert** folder then click **OK**.

In the **Choose Columns** dialog box, click the title of the **Clients** table to select it then click the ⟩ button. Confirm by clicking **Next**.
Click **Next** in the **Filter Data** and **Sort Order** dialog boxes.
In the **Finish** dialog box, activate the **Return Data to Microsoft Excel** option then click **Finish**.
Activate the **New worksheet** option in the **Returning External Data to Microsoft Excel** dialog box and click **OK**.

ANALYSIS TOOLS
Lesson 2.1: Auditing

1 ▪ Showing/hiding the Auditing toolbar

*The **Auditing** toolbar contains tools that allow you to highlight problems in your worksheets.*

▪ **Tools -Auditing**

▪ Click the **Show Auditing Toolbar** option to show or hide the **Auditing** toolbar.

If there is a tick to the left of the option, then the toolbar is already displayed.

*You can also hide the **Auditing** toolbar by clicking the* ⊠ *button, which is only visible when the toolbar is shown as a window (a floating toolbar).*

2 ▪ Showing errors

If an error value (e.g. #DIV/0!) appears in a cell as the result of a formula, it is possible to identify all the cells that provide the formula data.

▪ Click the cell that contains the error.

▪ Click the ⬦ tool on the **Auditing** toolbar.

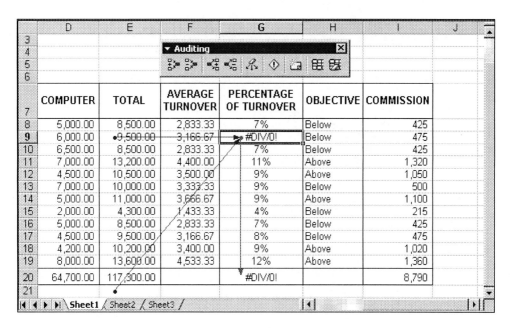

	D	E	F	G	H	I	J
	COMPUTER	TOTAL	AVERAGE TURNOVER	PERCENTAGE OF TURNOVER	OBJECTIVE	COMMISSION	
8	5,000.00	8,500.00	2,833.33	7%	Below	425	
9	6,000.00	9,500.00	3,166.67	#DIV/0!	Below	475	
10	6,500.00	8,500.00	2,833.33	7%	Below	425	
11	7,000.00	13,200.00	4,400.00	11%	Above	1,320	
12	4,500.00	10,500.00	3,500.00	9%	Above	1,050	
13	7,000.00	10,000.00	3,333.33	9%	Below	500	
14	5,000.00	11,000.00	3,666.67	9%	Above	1,100	
15	2,000.00	4,300.00	1,433.33	4%	Below	215	
16	5,000.00	8,500.00	2,833.33	7%	Below	425	
17	4,500.00	9,500.00	3,166.67	8%	Below	475	
18	4,200.00	10,200.00	3,400.00	9%	Above	1,020	
19	8,000.00	13,600.00	4,533.33	12%	Above	1,360	
20	64,700.00	117,300.00		#DIV/0!		8,790	
21							

Sheet1 / Sheet2 / Sheet3 /

Auditing arrows appear on the screen. Red arrows join the cell that has produced the error to those that refer to it, whereas blue arrows show the precedents of the erroneous cell.

 *To remove the auditing arrows, click the* 🔲 *tool on the **Auditing** toolbar.*

📖 3 ▪ Showing dependents

This command uses auditing arrows to hightlight the cells that contain a formula that refers to the selected cell.

▪ Select the cell concerned.

▪ **Tools - Auditing - Trace Dependents** or 🔲

ANALYSIS TOOLS
Lesson 2.1: Auditing

	D	E	F	G	H	I	J
3							
4			▼ Auditing		☒		
5							
6							
7	COMPUTER	TOTAL	AVERAGE TURNOVER	PERCENTAGE OF TURNOVER	OBJECTIVE	COMMISSION	
8	5,000.00	8,500.00	2,833.33	7%	Below	425	
9	6,000.00	9,500.00	3,166.67	#DIV/0!	Below	475	
10	6,500.00	8,500.00	2,833.33	7%	Below	425	
11	7,000.00	13,200.00	4,400.00	11%	Above	1,320	
12	4,500.00	10,500.00	3,500.00	9%	Above	1,050	
13	7,000.00	10,000.00	3,333.33	9%	Below	500	
14	5,000.00	11,000.00	3,666.67	9%	Above	1,100	
15	2,000.00	4,300.00	1,433.33	4%	Below	215	
16	5,000.00	8,500.00	2,833.33	7%	Below	425	
17	4,500.00	9,500.00	3,166.67	8%	Below	475	
18	4,200.00	10,200.00	3,400.00	9%	Above	1,020	
19	8,000.00	13,600.00	4,533.33	12%	Above	1,360	
20	64,700.00	117,300.00		#DIV/0!		8,790	
21							

Sheet1 / Sheet2 / Sheet3 /

The dependent cells are show with blue arrows.

※ To remove the dependent arrows, click the ⬛ tool on the **Auditing** toolbar.

📄 *To find the cells that refer to the dependent cells (show by blue arrows), click ⬛ again.*

🔲4 ▪ **Showing precedents**

This command uses auditing arrows to find cells used in formulas.

※ Select the cell that contains the formula.

※ **Tools - Auditing - Trace Precedents** or ⬛

	CURRENT YEAR	HI FI	VIDEO	COMPUTER	TOTAL	AVERAGE TURNOVER	PERCENTA OF TURNOV
8	January	1,000.00	2,500.00	5,000.00	8,500.00	2,833.33	7%
9	February	1,500.00	2,000.00	6,000.00	9,500.00	3,166.67	#DIV/0!
10	March	1,000.00	1,000.00	6,500.00	8,500.00	2,833.33	7%
11	April	1,200.00	5,000.00	7,000.00	13,200.00	4,400.00	11%
12	May	2,000.00	4,000.00	4,500.00	10,500.00	3,500.00	9%
13	June	1,500.00	1,500.00	7,000.00	10,000.00	3,333.33	9%
14	July	1,000.00	5,000.00	5,000.00	11,000.00	3,666.67	9%
15	August	800.00	1,500.00	2,000.00	4,300.00	1,433.33	4%
16	September	1,500.00	2,000.00	5,000.00	8,500.00	2,833.33	7%
17	October	2,000.00	3,000.00	4,500.00	9,500.00	3,166.67	8%
18	November	2,500.00	3,500.00	4,200.00	10,200.00	3,400.00	9%
19	December	1,600.00	4,000.00	8,000.00	13,600.00	4,533.33	12%
20	TOTAL	17,600.00	35,000.00	64,700.00	117,300.00		#DIV/0!

Sheet1 / Sheet2 / Sheet3 /

If the calculation formula contains a function, the precedent cells are framed and an arrow links them to the calculation formula; if not, only the auditing arrows appear.

▪ To remove the precedent arrows, click the 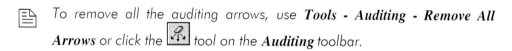 tool on the **Auditing** toolbar.

*To remove all the auditing arrows, use **Tools - Auditing - Remove All Arrows** or click the tool on the **Auditing** toolbar.*

When you make changes to a formula, the cells to which it refers are framed in the worksheet.

5 ▪ Analysing data

Excel provides you with several analysis tools with functions for analysing financial and statistical data.

▪ If necessary, load the **Analysis ToolPak** add-in. To do this, use **Tools - Add-Ins**, and in the **Add-Ins available** list, activate the check-box next to the **Analysis ToolPak** add-in, then click **OK**. If this add-in is not installed on your computer, Excel asks if you want to install it.

*The **Data Analysis** option is now available in the **Tools** menu.*

▪ **Tools - Data Analysis**

*The **Data Analysis** dialog box appears on screen:*

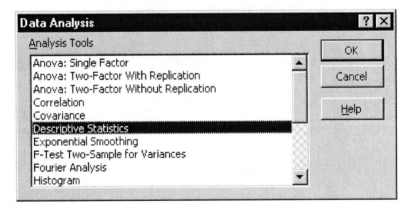

▪ Using the **Analysis Tools** list, choose the option you want.

▪ Click the **OK** button.

▪ Define the **Input** settings and the **Output Options** for the analysis.

▪ Click the **OK** button.

Below, you can see **Practice Exercise** 2.1. This exercise is made up of 5 steps. If you do not know how to complete one of the steps, go back to the lesson to refer to the corresponding title. When you have finished, check your work by reading the **Solution** on the next page.

All the steps in this exercise are likely to be tested in the exam.

Practice Exercise 2.1

*In order to complete exercise 2.1, you should open **2-1 Hi-FI.xls** in the **MOUS Excel 2000 Expert** folder then activate **Sheet 1**.*

1. Show the **Auditing** toolbar.

2. Using the auditing arrows, find all the cells that provide data for the formula in cell **G20**; in this cell the result of the formula is showing an error value.

3. Use auditing arrows to find the precedents of cell **E8**.

4. Use auditing arrows to find the precedents of cell **F8**, and then remove all the auditing arrows.

5. Using the **Descriptive Statistics** data analysis, display the statistics of cells **E8** to **E19**. These statistics should be arranged by **Column** and displayed as **Summary statistics**, in a new worksheet called **Stat**.

If you want to put what you have learned into practice in a real document, you can work on summary exercise 2 for the ANALYSIS TOOLS section that you can find at the end of this book.

It is often possible to perform a task in several different ways, but here only the quickest solution is presented. Go back to the lesson to see the other techniques that can be used.

 Solution to Exercise 2.1

1. Show the **Auditing** toolbar by running **Tools - Auditing**.
   Select the **Show Auditing Toolbar** command.

2. To use auditing arrows to find all the cells that supply data to the formula in cell G20, click in cell **G20** to select it.
   Click the ⟨image⟩ tool on the **Auditing** toolbar.

3. To find, using auditing arrows, all the dependents of cell E8, click in cell **E8** to select it. Click the ⟨image⟩ tool on the **Auditing** toolbar.

4. To show all of cell **F8**'s precedents, first click cell **F8** to select it. Click the ⟨image⟩ tool on the **Auditing** toolbar.
   Delete all the auditing arrows by clicking the ⟨image⟩ tool on the **Auditing** toolbar.

5. To display the statistics of cells **E8** to **E19** obtained using the data analysis tool **Descriptive Statistics**, in a new worksheet called **Stat**, use the **Tools - Data Analysis** command.
   In the **Analysis tools** list, select the **Descriptive Statistics** option then click **OK**.
   In the **Input** frame, click the ⟨image⟩ button in the **Input Range** box, select cells **E8** to **E19** and click the ⟨image⟩ button to redisplay the **Descriptive Statistics** dialog box then activate the **Columns** option.
   In the **Output Options** frame, activate the **New Worksheet Ply** option and type **Stat** in the corresponding text box then tick the **Summary statistics** option. Click the **OK** button.

ANALYSIS TOOLS
Lesson 2.2: Solver

1 ▪ Setting a goal value

This is a technique for working out problems like this are: what is the value a given cell must contain if a calculation result is to correspond to a goal value?

▪ Activate the cell that you wish to set to a certain value and ensure that it contains a calculation formula.

▪ If possible, show the cell containing the variable value in the same screen.

▪ **Tools - Goal Seek**

▪ Set the goal value in the **To value** box and indicate the variable cell in **By changing cell**.

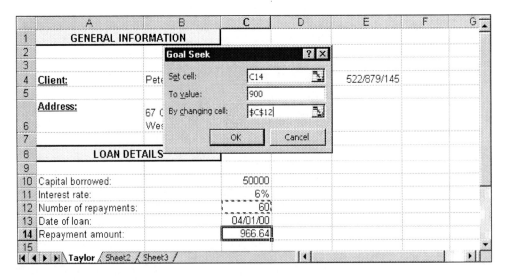

How many repayments will have to be made for the monthly repayment amount to equal 900?

▪ Click **OK**.

As soon as Excel finds a solution, it stops searching and displays its results on the screen.

* If you are satisfied with the result offered, click **OK** to keep it on the worksheet. To return to the original values, click **Cancel**.

2 ▪ Solving a problem with variables and multiple constraints

* If necessary, install the **Solver** add-in.

  *The **Solver** option becomes available in the **Tools** menu.*

Entering the problem data

* **Tools - Solver**
* In **Set Target Cell**, specify the cell for which you are setting a target value.
* In **Equal To**, indicate whether the cell is to be maximised (**Max**), minimised (**Min**) or set to a specific value (**Value of**).
* Next, specify the cells containing the values that can be varied in the **By Changing Cells** box.

Managing constraints

* To create constraints, click **Add** then, for each one, activate the cell concerned and specify the constraint.
  Continue adding constraints in the same way, using the **Add** button; when you have finished your list of constraints, click **OK**.

For example:

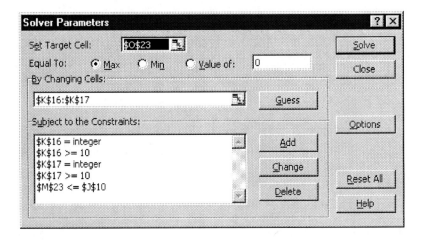

You can select constraints and use the **Delete** or **Change** buttons to remove or edit them.

Starting the solving process

» Click the **Solve** button.

Various messages appear on the status bar, then Excel tells you that a solution has been found and displays it on the worksheet.

» Click **Save Scenario** to save the solution found by Solver. Give the scenario a name then click **OK**.

» If you are satisfied with the result obtained, click **Keep Solver Solution**, otherwise choose to **Restore Original Values**.

» Click **OK**.

*To remove all the elements of a problem, go into the **Solver Parameters** dialog box (**Tools - Solver**), click the **Reset All** button then click **OK** to confirm.*

▣3 ▪ Saving/loading problem parameters

Saving a Solver model

▪ On the sheet, activate the top left cell in the range reserved for the model.

▪ **Tools - Solver**

▪ If necessary, set out the problem you want to save.

▪ Click the **Options** button, then **Save Model**.

▪ If necessary, modify the range reserved for the model in **Select Model Area** and click **OK**.

▪ Click **OK** to confirm the **Solver Options** dialog box then close the **Solver Parameters** dialog box by clicking **Close**.

 A model is a collection of logical values.

Loading a model

▪ **Tools - Solver**

▪ Click the **Options** button then click **Load Model**.

▪ Select the range reserved for the model then click **OK**.

▪ Confirm the request to use the model with **OK** then click **OK** again to close the options window.

In this way, all the elements of the problem are retrieved.

▣4 ▪ Making scenarios

A scenario enables you to solve a problem by considering several hypotheses.

Creating scenarios

▪ **Tools - Scenarios**

▪ For each scenario to create:

- Click **Add**.

- Enter the **Scenario name** in the corresponding text box.

- Delete whatever appears in the **Changing cells** box, click the 🔲 button and hold down ⌷Ctrl⌷ while you select on the sheet the cells whose values should vary in this scenario.

- Click the 🔲 button to restore the **Add Scenario** dialog box then click **OK**.

- Enter the values for each changing cell and click **OK**.

Using a scenario

▪ **Tools - Scenarios**

▪ If you only want to run one scenario, select it, click **Show** then click the **Close** button. The result replaces the current values on the worksheet (this is why you should start by creating a scenario containing the current values).

If you want to run a summary report of all the scenarios, click **Summary** then, in the **Result cells box,** enter the cell references (or select the cells) whose results interest you.

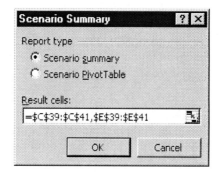

* Click **OK**.

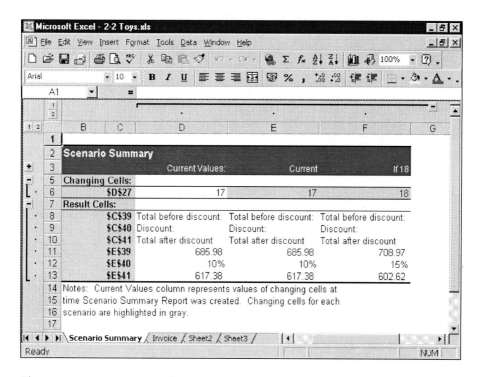

The summary is presented as an outline on a separate worksheet.

📄 *Scenarios and views can be associated in a report.*

Below you can see **Practice Exercise** 2.2. This exercise is made up of 4 steps. If you do not know how to complete one of the steps, go back to the lesson to refer to the corresponding title. When you have finished, check your work by reading the **Solution** on the next page.

All the steps in this exercise are likely to be tested in the exam.

☞ **Practice Exercise 2.2**

1. On the **Taylor** sheet of the **2-2 Loan.xls** workbook, in the **MOUS Excel 2000 Expert** folder, find which value **C12** (monthly repayments) should contain in order for the repayment amount in **C14** to equal 900.

2. On the **January** sheet in the **2-2 Assembly Line.xls** workbook in the **MOUS Excel 2000 Expert** folder, use the Solver to calculate the optimal profit possible (in cell O23), by changing the number of units produced. Take into account these constraints:
   - total hours (cell M23) < = available hours (cell J10).
   - number of tractors > = 10
   - number of vans > = 10
   - the number of tractors and vans must be whole numbers (no decimals).

   You do not need to create any scenario or any report.

3. Save the problem model on the **January** sheet in the **2-2 Assembly Line.xls** workbook in the **MOUS Excel 2000 Expert** folder; the first cell in the model area should be cell **A31**.
   Next, load the model of problem 2 (cells B31 to B38) in the **January** sheet and start the Solver.

4. Create two scenarios on the **Invoice** sheet of the **2-2 Toys.xls** workbook in the **MOUS Excel 2000 Expert** folder: the current scenario (17 giant lions sold), called **Current** and another with a quantity of 18 lions sold, called **If 18**.

If the **Total before discount** (E31) is more than 700, the discount accorded is 15%. On this invoice, the client has missed out on the maximum discount because only 17 giant lions were ordered. Using these scenarios, you can see the difference in total price, had 18 of these toys been ordered. Start running both these scenarios in order to make a summary of their results on a new sheet.

If you want to put what you have learnt into practice on a real document, you can work on summary exercise 2 for the ANALYSIS TOOLS section, that you can find at the end of this book.

It is often possible to perform a task in several different ways, but here only the quickest solution is presented. Go back to the lesson to see the other techniques that can be used.

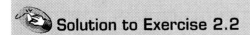

Solution to Exercise 2.2

1. To discover, on the Taylor sheet of the 2-2 Loan.xls workbook, what value cell C12 should contain in order for the repayments in cell C14 to equal 900, open the **2-2 Loan.xls** workbook and click the **Taylor** sheet tab.
   Click cell **C14** then use the **Tools - Goal Seek** comamnd.
   Enter **900** in the **To value** text box.
   Click the 🔲 button in the **By changing cell** box then click cell **C12**. Click the 🔲 button to restore the **Goal Seek** dialog box then click **OK**.

   Click **OK** to close the **Goal Seek Status** dialog box and apply the changes made to the **Taylor** worksheet.
   If you wish you can save the changes made to the **2-2 Loan.xls** workbook.

2. To use the Solver to optimise the total profits (cell O23) on the January sheet of the 2-2 Assembly Line.xls workbook, by changing the number of units produced and taking into account the constraints given (step 2 of the exercise), open the **2-2 Assemble Line.xls** workbook and activate the **January** sheet.
   Click cell **O23** then use the **Tools - Solver** command.
   If necessary, define the cell for which you are setting a target (**Set Target Cell**). To do this, click the 🔲 button, click cell **O23** then click the 🔲 button to restore the **Solver Parameters** dialog box.
   Leave the **Max** option active.

   Click the 🔲 button on the **By Changing Cells** box, select cells **K16** and **K17** then click the 🔲 button to restore the **Solver Parameters** dialog box again.

To create the constraint **total hours<=available hours**, click the **Add** button in the **Subject to the Constraints** frame.

Click the 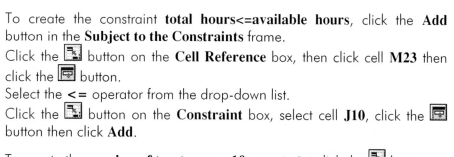 button on the **Cell Reference** box, then click cell **M23** then click the button.

Select the **<=** operator from the drop-down list.

Click the button on the **Constraint** box, select cell **J10**, click the button then click **Add**.

To create the **number of tractors > = 10**, constraint click the button on the **Cell Reference** box, then click cell **K16** then click the button.

Select the **>=** operator from the drop-down list.

Click the **Constraint** box, enter **10** then click the **Add** button.

To create the constraint **number of vans> = 10**, click the button on the **Cell Reference** box, click cell **K17** then click the button.

Select the **>=** operator from the dropdown list.

Click the **Constraints** box, enter **10** then click the **Add** button.

To create a constraint so the number of tractors is a whole number (no decimals), click the button on the **Cell Reference** box, click cell **K16** then click the button.

Select the **int** (integer) operator in the drop-down list then click **Add**.

To create a constraint so the number of vans is a whole number (no decimals), click the button on the **Cell Reference** box, click cell **K17** then click the button.

Select the **int** operator in the drop-down list then click **OK**.

Click the **Solve** button, leave the **Keep Solver Solution** option active then click **OK**.

3. To save the problem model from the January sheet in the 2-2 Assembly Line.xls workbook, open the **2-2 Assembly Line.xls** workbook then click the **January** tab.

Click cell **A31** then use the **Tools - Solver** command.

Click the **Options** button, the **Save Model** button then click **OK**.

Click **OK** to confirm the **Solver Options** dialog box then close the **Solver Parameters** dialog box by clicking **Close**.

To load the model of problem 2 (cells B31 to B38) in the January sheet then solve it, activate the **January** sheet tab and use the **Tools - Solver** command.

Click the **Options** button then click **Load Model**.

Click the 🔙 button then select cells **A31** to **A38**.

Click the 🔲 button then click **OK**.

Use **OK** to confirm the request to use the model then click **OK** again to close the **Solver Options** dialog box.

Click the **Solve** button then click **OK**.

4. In order to create two scenarios from the Invoice sheet on the 2-2 Toys.xls workbook, open the **2-2 Toys.xls** workbook in the **MOUS Excel 2000 Expert** folder, click the **Invoice** tab then use the **Tools - Scenarios** command.

To create a scenario that would keep the current values, click the **Add** button then type **Current** in the **Scenario name** box.

Click the 🔙 button on the **Changing cells** box, click cell **D27** then click the 🔲 button.

Click **OK**, keep **17** in the only text box available then click **OK**.

To create a scenario that would show a quantity of 18 giant lions, click the **Add** button then enter **If 18** as the **Scenario name**.

Keep reference **D27** in the **Changing cells** box then click **OK**.

Enter **18** in the text box then click **OK** and finally click **Close**.

To run the scenarios and create a summary of them on a new sheet, use the **Tools - Scenarios** comamnd then click the **Summary** button.

Leave the **Scenario summary** option active, click the button, select cells **C39** to **C41** and cells **E39** to **E41** then click .

Click **OK** to confirm then if you wish, save the changes made to the **2-2 Toys.xls** workbook.

ANALYSIS TOOLS
Exercise 2.2: Solver

ANALYSIS TOOLS
Lesson 2.3: Pivot table

▣1 ▪ **Creating a pivot table report**

A pivot table allows you to synthesise and analyse data from a list or existing table:

	A	B	C	D	E	F	
1	Sales ID	(All)	▼				
2							
3	Average of Units Sold	Date	▼				
4	Region	▼	Jan	Feb	Mar	Apr	Grand Total
5	Central		109	128	129	119	119
6	East		130	110	129	139	126
7	North		142	152	111	169	146
8	South		112	129	148	134	130
9	West		136	126	127	117	127
10	Grand Total		123	129	132	132	129
11							

In this example, the pivot table calculates the average unit sales by region and by date.

▪ **Data - PivotTable and PivotChart Report** or ⊡

*The **PivotTable and PivotChart Wizard** appears on the screen.*

▪ Indicate the location of the data you wish to analyse with the pivot table: if the source data is in a database, leave the first option active.

▪ If necessary, leave the **PivotTable** option active under **What kind of report do you want to create?**

▪ Click **Next**.

▪ Select the range of cells containing the data used to fill in the table (this could be the entire database).

▪ Click **Next**.

⁑ Click the **Layout** button then define the table's design by dragging the field buttons from the list into the appropriate areas (ROW, COLUMN, DATA, PAGE). The field placed in the PAGE area is used to display a synthesis of all the elements in that field or to show them one by one.

⁑ For example:

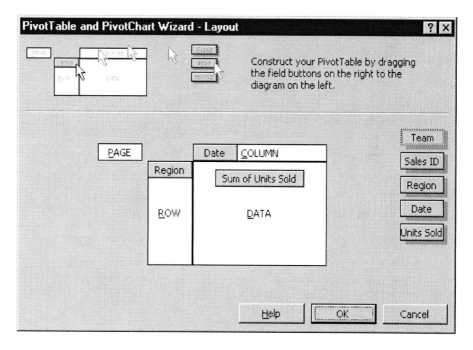

*This pivot table is designed to calculate the sum of Units Sold by Region and by Date. The **DATA** area can only contain elements that Excel can calculate.*

⁑ If necessary, customise the fields included in the table by double-clicking the corresponding field button. If for example, you wish to make a calculation other than a sum, click the **Sum** button in the DATA area then choose another function. Confirm your choice with **OK**.

⁑ Click **OK** on the **Wizard** dialog box.

※ Under **Where do you want to put the PivotTable**, indicate whether you want to create it on a **New worksheet** or on an **Existing worksheet** (in which case, give the worksheet name).

※ Click the **Finish** button.

The pivot table and the Pivot Table toolbar appear on the screen.

📄 *Although a pivot table is linked to the list that is the source of its data, it can only be updated manually.*

📖2 ▪ Modifying a pivot table report

Modifying fields

※ Click in the pivot table.

※ **Data - PivotTable and PivotChart Report** or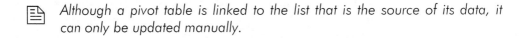

※ Click the **Layout** button.

※ Redefine the contents of the table, as you did when it was created. To delete a field, drag the field concerned out of the area containing it.

※ Click **OK** then **Finish**.

📄 *A field can also be added by dragging the corresponding button from the **PivotTable** toolbar onto the table. To delete a field, drag it off the pivot table.*

Modifying the data used for the calculation

» Click the down arrow that appears to the right of each field name:

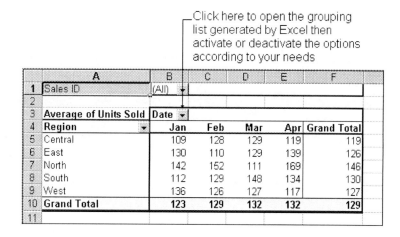

Click here to open the grouping list generated by Excel then activate or deactivate the options according to your needs

	A	B	C	D	E	F
1	Sales ID	(All) ▼				
2						
3	Average of Units Sold	Date ▼				
4	Region ▼	Jan	Feb	Mar	Apr	Grand Total
5	Central	109	128	129	119	119
6	East	130	110	129	139	126
7	North	142	152	111	169	146
8	South	112	129	148	134	130
9	West	136	126	127	117	127
10	Grand Total	123	129	132	132	129
11						

» Activate (or deactivate) the values you wish to include in (or remove from) the table.

» Click **OK**.

Recalculating values

If the source data have been modified, you should refresh the pivot table to update the values it displays.

» **Data - Refresh Data** or [⭥]

Modifying its presentation

» The cells on a pivot table can be formatted in the same way as those on an ordinary table. You can also apply an AutoFormat to the entire table, using the **Format - AutoFormat** command (see below).

3 ▪ Applying an AutoFormat to a pivot table

❋ Click a cell in the pivot table.

❋ **Format - AutoFormat**

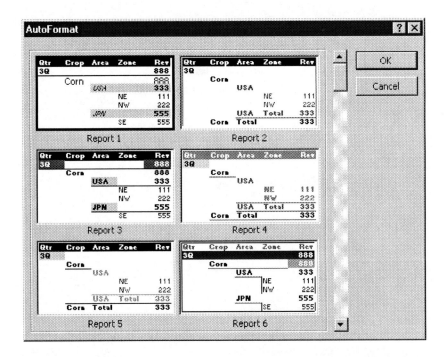

❋ From the range of models shown, choose the one that suits you best.

*The **None** model, shown at the end of the list, deletes all formatting from the cells in the table but keeps the arrangement of rows and columns as defined in the last Autoformat applied.*

❋ Confirm by clicking **OK** then click outside the pivot table to view the result.

▥4 ▪ Grouping rows or columns in a pivot table

*This function allows you to group a **Dates** field by month, for example.*

▪ Click the name of the field which you intend to group the data.

▪ **Data - Group and Outline - Group**

▪ Indicate how the data should be grouped.

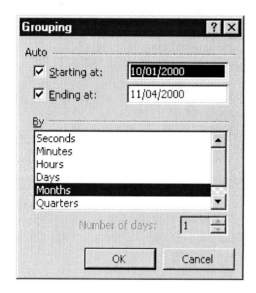

The dates here will be grouped together by month.

▪ Click **OK**.

▪ To cancel the grouping, use the command **Data - Group and Outline - Ungroup**.

5 ▪ Creating an interactive pivot table in a Web page

An Excel pivot table can be published in an Internet or intranet site. If you want to create an interactive pivot table, which visitors to the site can modify, you should publish the pivot table as an interactive list, by following the procedure set out in this lesson.

*To publish this type of Web page, you need to have installed Internet Explorer 4.01 (or later version) as well as the relevant component for managing **pivot table lists**. This is only available in the browser if the Microsoft Office Web Components are installed on your computer.*

Internet or intranet users who wish to change the layout or data shown in the Web page have to also have these elements installed on their computers.

⬚ Create or open the sheet in which the pivot table appears. This sheet will be saved in html format (a whole workbook cannot be interactive).

⬚ **File - Save As Web Page**

⬚ Select the name of the folder (Web or local) and the Web server in the **Save in** list.

*Depending on your choice, Excel may prompt you to give a user name and password in order to access the selected server. If this is the case, fill in the appropriate text boxes and confirm by clicking **OK**.*

⬚ Activate the **Selection: sheet** option and check the **Add interactivity** box.

⬚ Click the **Change Title** button to enter the text that will appear as a title above the published selection then confirm with **OK**.

⬚ Type the **File name** in the corresponding text box (by default, the name will be **Page.htm**).

⬚ Click the **Publish** button.

» Under **Items to publish**, activate **PivotTable** in the second list box.

» In the **Add interactivity with** list, choose the Excel functionality you wish to put at the user's disposal. Choose the appropriate function depending on the element you are publishing, in this case **PivotTable functionality**.

» To view the Web page in the default browser as soon as it has been published, activate the **Open published web page in browser** option.

» Click **Publish**.

» If necessary, give your access name and password for the server.

Your browser may inform you that the source data for the pivot table are located in another domain. In this case, click Yes to continue.

Excel publishes the Web page on the chosen server and simultaneously saves the file in htm format, along with a folder containing its supporting files. In this way, Web page files are stored exclusively on the server; only the source file is located on your hard disk.

The Internet Explorer browser automatically presents the list of data published in a pivot table form. Each field has a drop-down list containing its details. It is possible to activate or deactivate various elements in order to modify the pivot table. A user visiting this page can easily change what the pivot table displays, without actually having the Excel application, as this operation is performed directly in the browser!

It is not possible to have a **Web Page Preview** when the page is interactive. To view an interactive page, activate the **Open published web page in browser** option in the **Publish as Web Page** dialog box (**File - Save As Web Page - Publish**).

6 ▪ Using a pivot table list in a Web browser

What is a pivot table list?

▪ A **PivotTable list** is an interactive table that you can use to analyse data, within a Web browser. This table is made up of elements on which it is possible to use commands and features similar to those used in an Excel pivot table report.

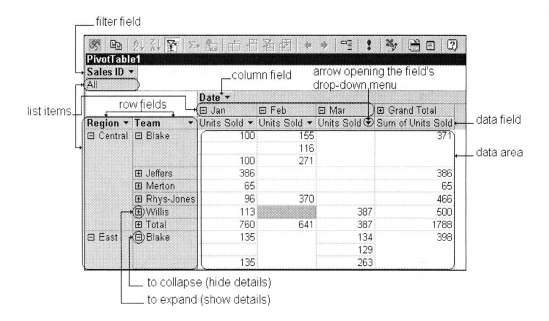

Displaying data in a pivot table list

A pivot table list in a Web page contains similar commands and features to those in an Excel pivot table report.

▪ You can modify the layout and data shown by using the corresponding toolbar.

ANALYSIS TOOLS
Lesson 2.3: Pivot table

Here is a description of the **PivotTable List** toolbar:

1. Shows the About Microsoft Office Web Components dialog box.

2. Copies the data selected in the pivot table list into the clipboard.

3. Sorts the data in the selected field in ascending order.

4. Sorts the data in the selected field in descending order.

5. Activates or deactivates filtering on all fields.

6. Adds a total field to the field list, by summarizing the data with the Sum, Min, Max or Count function.

7. Displays or hides the sub-totals in the selected field.

8. Moves the selected field so it becomes a row field.

9. Moves the selected field so it becomes a column field.

10. Moves the selected field so it becomes a filter field.

11. Moves the selected field to the detail area so that the data in the field are not summarised.

12. Promote the selected row field or inside column by one level towards the outside of the table.

13. Demote the selected row field or outside column by one level towards the inside of the table.

14. Shows or hides all the details of the field, element or cell selected in the data area.

15. Updates the pivot table list using the source file or database

16. Copies the pivot table list into a new Excel workbook as a pivot table report.

17. Opens the pivot table Properties toolbox.

18. Shows the list of available fields using the pivot table list source data.

19. Shows help topics.

Modifying what a pivot table list shows

- To hide a field's details, click the corresponding ⊟ sign and to expand the details again, click the ⊞ sign.

- To display or hide the elements in a column field, click the drop-down list on the field name then activate the field values you want to display or deactivate the ones you want to hide. Confirm your choice by clicking **OK**.

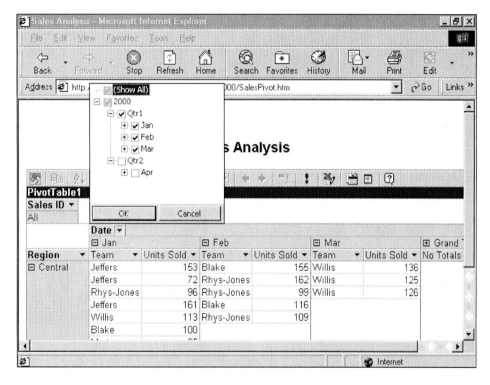

The "Date" field shown here is made up of various levels. On this example, only the months of January, February and March 2000 (or the first quarter of that year) are displayed.

Deleting a field from a pivot table list

▪ To delete a field from a pivot table list, point to the name of the field concerned, (the mouse pointer is accompanied by a four-headed arrow) then drag the field off the pivot table. Release the mouse button when a red cross ☒ appears with the pointer.

The field is deleted from the pivot table list but not from the source data. the pivot table list is modified instantly.

Adding a field to a pivot table list

▪ To add a field to a pivot table list from the source data, click the ▣ tool to see a list of the available fields.

▪ Click the element you want to move to the pivot table list.

▪ Open the drop down list at the bottom of the **PivotTable Field List** dialog box then choose where you want to insert the selected field: in the **Row Area**, **Column Area**, **Filter Area**, **Data Area** or the **Detail Data**.

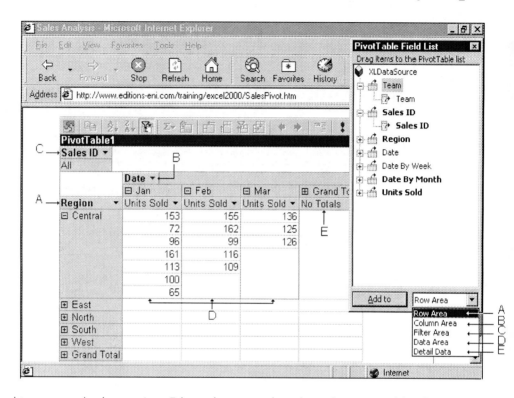

On this screen, the letters A to E have been used to show the pivot table element which corresponds to each option.

⁘ Click the **Add to** button.

📄 *By default, a data field (**Data Area**) summarizes numerical data with the Sum function and non-numerical data with the Count function.*

Adding a total field to a pivot table list

⁘ Click the field whose values you wish to summarize.

⁘ Click the ⎣Σ▾⎦ tool, called **AutoCalc** and choose the option appropriate to the operation you want to perform (**Sum**, **Count**, **Min** or **Max**).

Open the list of available fields by clicking the tool: you notice there is now a new folder called **Totals** in which you can see all the possible total fields.

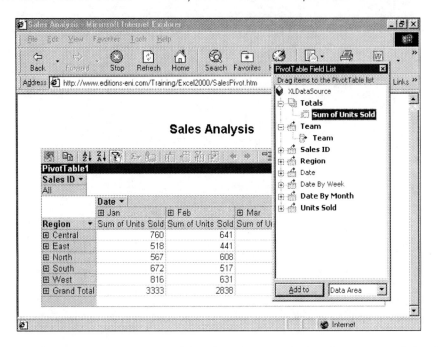

The <u>total field</u> takes the name of the function used plus the name of the field (**Sum of Units Sold**).

To delete a total field from the data source, open the list of available fields, RIGHT-click the field concerned and click the **Delete** option. You can however delete a total field from the pivot table list in the same way you would for an ordinary field

Any changes made to the pivot table list are only saved for the duration of your session. If you open the Web page again, for example by clicking the address bar on the browser and pressing the ⏎ key, the changes you previously made will have disappeared.

Below you can see **Practice Exercise** 2.3. This exercise is made up of 6 steps. If you do not know how to complete one of the steps, go back to the lesson to refer to the corresponding title. When you have finished, check your work by reading the **Solution** on the next page.

All the steps in this exercise are likely to be tested in the exam.

☞ Practice Exercise 2.3

*In order to complete exercise 2.3, you should open the **2-3 Team Sales.xls** workbook located in the **MOUS Excel 2000 Expert** folder.*

🖼 1. On a new worksheet, create the pivot table shown below from the data contained in the **2-3 Team Sales.xls** workbook:

	A	B	K	L	M	N	O	P
1	Team	(All)						
2								
3	Sum of Units Sold	Date						
4	Region	10/01/2000	13/03/2000	20/03/2000	27/03/2000	03/04/2000	10/04/2000	Grand Total
5	Central	153		261	126	116	478	2382
6	East	142	114	98	297	163	255	2020
7	North	232	102		119	185	323	1904
8	South	127	175		270	253	284	2465
9	West	158		205	152	392	192	2540
10	Grand Total	812	391	564	964	1109	1532	11311
11								

This pivot table report represents the sum of the units sold by region and by date, for all the sales teams (here, columns C to J have been masked so you can see the Grand Total column).

🖼 2. Modify the pivot table report so you have a report which can be produced for each **Sales ID** insead of for each **Team** and that the results shown are an **Average** and not a **Sum**.

3. Apply the AutoFormat called **Table 4** to your pivot table report.

4. Show the sales averages by **month** and without decimals points.

5. Publish your pivot table as an interactive Web page. If you do not have access rights to the Internet or an intranet, you can still publish your pivot table in the **My Documents** folder on your hard disk.

6. If you have Internet Explorer (version 4.01 or later) display the Web page: http://www.editions-eni.com/training/EXCEL2000/SalesPivot.htm. Modify the pivot table so you obtain the result shown below:

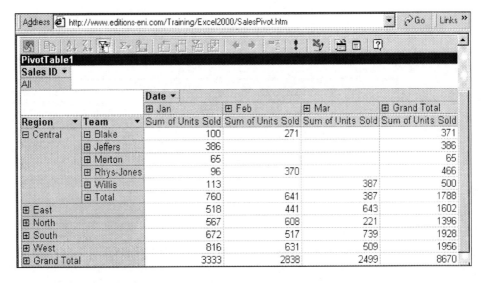

To obtain this result, you must:
- display just the first quarter results in the **Date** field.
- delete the **Team** field from the Detail Data.
- make a Sum calculation (AutoCalc) on the **Units Sold** field.
- add the **Team** field to the Row Area.

If you want to put what you have learnt into practice on a real document, you can work on summary exercise 2 for the ANALYSIS TOOLS section, that you can find at the end of this book.

It is often possible to perform a task in several different ways, but here only the quickest solution is presented. Go back to the lesson to see the other techniques that can be used.

Solution to Exercise 2.3

 1. To make a pivot table report like the one shown in the exercise, click one of the cells in the list of data in the **2-3 Team Sales** workbook (Vendors sheet).
Use the **Data - PivotTable and PivotChart Report** command.
If necessary, activate the **Microsoft Excel list or database** and **PivotTable** options before clicking the **Next** button.
Make sure the cell range listed as the data source is: **$A$1:$E$89** then click **Next**.
If necessary, activate the **New worksheet** option then click the **Layout** button.
Drag the names of the **Date**, **Team**, **Region** and **Units Sold** fields onto the appropriate areas, referring to the model below:

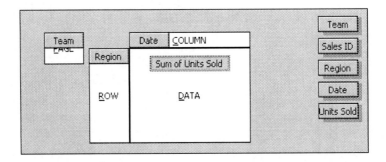

The Sum function is the default function attributed to the DATA field.

Click **OK** on the **Layout** dialog box.
Click **Finish** to create the pivot table report, on a new worksheet.

▣ 2. To replace the Team field with the Sales ID field, activate a cell in the pivot table then click the 🔲 tool on the **PivotTable** toolbar. Click the **Layout** button then drag the **Team** field from the PAGE area and replace it with the **Sales ID** field.

To change the **Sum** function on the **Units Sold** field, double-click the **Sum of Units Sold** field button, choose the **Average** function in the **Summarize by** dropdown list then click **OK**.
Confirm the changes made in the **Layout** dialog box by clicking **OK**.

Close the Wizard, confirming your work by clicking the **Finish** button.

▣ 3. To apply an AutoFormat to the Pivot Table report, activate one of the cells in the pivot table then use the **Format - AutoFormat** command.
Using the vertical scroll bar, scroll through the models then click the **Table 4** model.
Click **OK** to confirm your choice.

▣ 4. To show the average sales per month, click the heading of the **Date** field on the pivot table then use the **Data - Group and Outline - Group** command.
Choose the **Month'**option in the **By** list then click **OK**.

To change the format of cells on a pivot table, use the same features as for an ordinary table. Start by selecting all the result cells (from **B5** to **F10**), then click the 🔲 tool on the **Formatting** toolbar as many times as is necessary to remove all the decimal places.

5. To publish your pivot table, use the **File - Save As Web Page** command.

In this example, the Web page will be published on the hard disk but you can adapt the parameters if you have the chance to publish Web pages on an Internet or intranet server.

Using the **Save in** list, choose the location where the data will be stored (or use the **Web Folders** shortcut if you have access to a network).
Activate the **Selection: sheet** option then click the **Add interactivity** box. Click the **Change Title** button and enter **Sales Analysis** (this text will appear above the data as a title for the table).

Confirm the title with **OK**.

In the **File name** box, delete the present contents (Page.htm) then enter the file name **SalesPivot.htm** (you do not have to enter the .htm file extension if you do not want to). Click the **Publish** button.

Select **PivotTable: PivotTable 1...** in the second list under **Items to publish**.
Make sure the **Add interactivity with: PivotTable functionality** and the **Open published web page in browser** options are both active.
Click the **Publish** button.

*The Internet Explorer browser opens and displays the Web page, indicating the **Address** (path) for the new Web page.*

6. To change the pivot table as described in the exercise, from the browser itself, you should first open the Internet Explorer browser, then go to the Web page located at this address: http://www.editions-eni.com/training/EXCEL2000/SalesPivot.htm.

To change the way the **Date** field is displayed, click the down arrow attached to this field, then click the ⊞ sign to the left of the year **2000** to show the corresponding values. Deactivate the **Qtr2** option (for the second quarter).

Click **OK** to confirm your modification.

To delete one of the data fields, start by displaying them all by clicking the ⊞ sign to the left of one of the row fields, for the **Central** region for example. By doing this, you will show the **Team** and **Units Sold** fields. Drag the **Team** field off the table to delete it from the pivot table list.

To make an automatic Sum calculation on the Units Sold field, click one of the headings in the **Units Sold** field then click the [Σ▾] tool. Next, click the **Sum** function.

To add a field to the pivot table list from the source data, click the 🖼 tool to show a list of all the available fields. Click the **Team** name to select it. Open the drop-down list at the bottom of the **PivotTable List** dialog box to select where you want to insert the new field, in this case in the **Row Area**.

Click the **Add to** button.

Click the ⊞ sign on the **Central** region to display the table exactly how it is shown in the practice exercise.

ANALYSIS TOOLS
Lesson 2.4: Pivot chart

ANALYSIS TOOLS
Lesson 2.4: Pivot chart

1 ▪ Creating a pivot chart

A pivot chart is always associated with a pivot table. Any changes made to the pivot table are carried over into the pivot chart and vice versa.

Several different methods exist for creating pivot charts, which vary depending on the source of the data you are using. It is possible to create a pivot chart from a range of Excel cells and to generate, at the same time, a corresponding pivot table. In this lesson, the pivot chart will be created directly from an existing pivot table.

▪ Go to the pivot table that is your data source.

▪ Click the ▦ tool on the **PivotTable** toolbar.

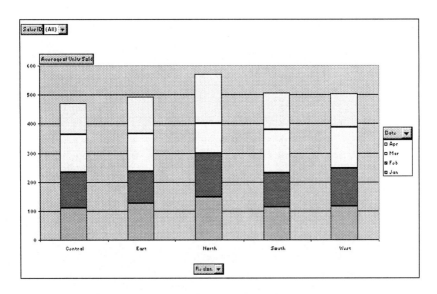

A stacked column chart (which is the default type) is created automatically on a chart sheet. The data on the rows of the pivot table become the chart categories and the data from the pivot table columns become the chart series.

*The **PivotChart (with PivotTable)** option you see when you use the **Data - PivotTable and PivotChart Report** command can be used to create a pivot chart with, as its source, an Excel, Access or OLAP database, or a simple range of Excel cells. In all these cases, a pivot table will be generated at the same time as the pivot chart.*

*To move a pivot chart's legend, choose one of the options in **Chart - Chart Options - Legend** tab. The legend cannot be moved or resized with the mouse.*
The titles on a pivot chart and its axes cannot be moved but you can change their size by changing the font or font size of the characters.

2 ▪ Displaying/hiding chart data

Displaying/hiding certain values

▪ Open the list corresponding to the field concerned and deactivate or activate the option that corresponds to the data you want to hide or display.

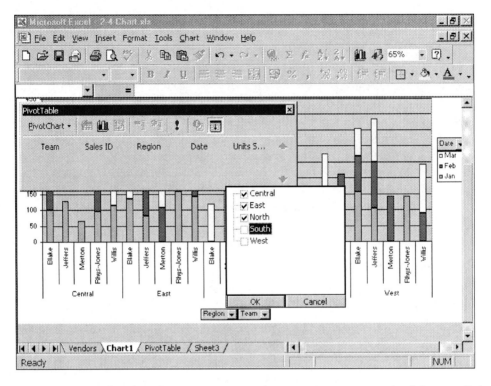

On this example, the data concerning three regions, instead of five, will be displayed simultaneously in the pivot chart and the corresponding pivot table.

» Click **OK**.

Adding/deleting a pivot chart field

» To add a field, drag it from the **PivotTable** toolbar onto the chart. If the toolbar cannot be seen, you can display it by choosing **View - Toolbars - PivotTable**.

» To delete a field, drag the field button off the chart.

3 ▪ Changing the pivot chart type

▪ Select the chart area.

▪ **Chart - Chart Type**

▪ Select a type then a **Chart sub-type**.

▪ Click **OK**.

> The **Scatter**, **Bubble** and **Stock** chart types cannot be used on pivot charts.

4 ▪ Moving a pivot chart to an existing sheet

▪ Activate the chart sheet and select the pivot chart.

▪ **Chart - Location**

▪ Click the **As object in** option and give the name of the sheet to which you want to move the chart.

▪ Click **OK.**

When a pivot chart is moved, it may lose some of its formatting parameters. The original chart sheet is deleted.

Below you can see **Practice Exercise** 2.4. This exercise is made up of 4 steps. If you do not know how to complete one of the steps, go back to the lesson to refer to the corresponding title. When you have finished, check your work by reading the **Solution** on the next page.

Steps that are likely to be tested on the exam are marked with a ▦ symbol. It is however recommended that you follow the whole exercise in order to gain a complete understanding of the lesson.

☞ Practice Exercise 2.4

*In order to complete exercise 2.4, you should open the **2-4 Chart.xls** workbook in the **MOUS Excel 2000 Expert** folder.*

▦ 1. On a new sheet in the **2-4 Chart.xls** workbook, create a pivot chart based on the model below:

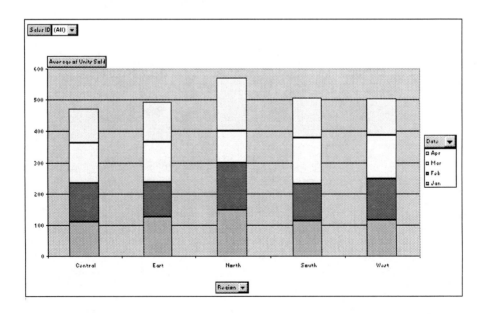

2. Display the average sales for the first quarter and add the **Team** field to the category axis, to obtain the result below:

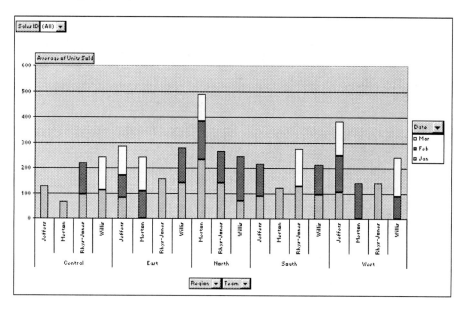

3. Change the pivot chart type to a **Clustered Column** type.

4. Move the pivot chart to the right of the pivot table located on the **PivotTable** worksheet then change the object size so the chart can be seen clearly.

If you want to put what you have learnt into practice on a real document, you can work on summary exercise 2 for the ANALYSIS TOOLS section, that you can find at the end of this book.

ANALYSIS TOOLS
Exercise 2.4: Pivot chart

It is often possible to perform a task in several different ways, but here only the quickest solution is presented. Go back to the lesson to see the other techniques that can be used.

Solution to Exercise 2.4

 1. To create a pivot chart from the pivot table in the 2-4 Chart.xls workbook, click the **PivotTable** sheet tab if necessary then, if the **PivotTable** toolbar cannot be seen, display it with the **View - Toolbars - PivotTable** command.

   Activate one of the cells in the pivot table then click the 📊 tool on the **PivotTable** toolbar.

   *A new sheet (**Chart1**) is created, containing a pivot chart of the Stacked Column type.*

2. To show only the sales averages for the first quarter, open the drop-down list on the **Date** field, then deactivate the **Apr** (April) value and click **OK**.
   To add the **Team** field to the right of the **Region** field on the category axis, display the **PivotTable** toolbar (if it is hidden) so you can see all the available fields.
   Drag the **Team** field from the toolbar onto the pivot chart, to the right of the **Region** field button. Release the mouse button when the symbol ▓▓ appears to the right of the **Region** field button.

3. To change the pivot chart type to a Clustered Column type, use the **Chart - Chart Type** command.
   Leave the **Column type** as **Column** then click the first sub-type, called **Clustered Column**.
   Click **OK**.

4. To move the pivot chart onto the PivotTable worksheet, select the pivot chart then use the **Chart - Location** command.

Activate the **As object in** option and select **PivotTable** from the list attached to this option.

Click **OK** then move the object to the right of the pivot table.

To change the object's size, click the object then drag the appropriate selection handles (the small black squares arround its edges) until you can see the chart correctly.

TEMPLATES, WORKBOOKS AND WORKGROUPS
Lesson 3.1: Templates

1 ▪ Creating a template

A template is a document that contains presentations, data... that can be used when you create new workbooks.

▪ Create the template document by deleting everything that does not need to be repeated in new workbooks and by activating any necessary protections.

▪ **File - Save As**.

▪ Open the **Save as type** list and click the **Template (*.xlt)** option.

▪ Indicate the name of the template in the **File name** box.

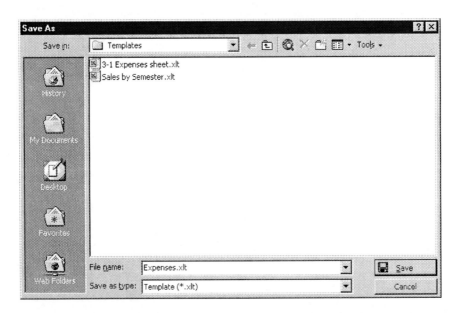

*Excel proposes to save the template in the folder called **Templates**.*

▪ If necessary, select another folder or sub-folder in the **Templates** folder.

▪ Click **Save**.

The extension given to templates is XLT.

⊞2 ▪ **Modifying a template**

To modify a template, you must first open it.

▪ **File - Open** or ⊞ or Ctrl O

▪ Select the folder in which the templates are stored (by default **C:\Windows\Application Data\Microsoft\Templates**).

▪ Open the **Files of type** drop-down list and click the **Templates (*.xlt)** option.

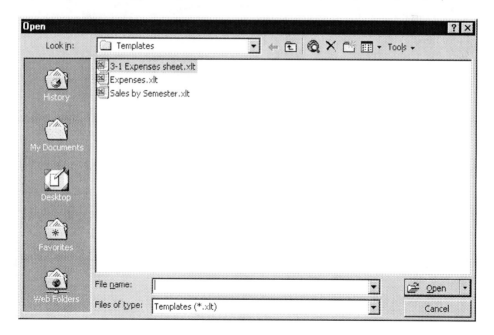

*Now the templates are visible in the **Open** dialog box.*

▪ Double-click the name of the template you want to open or select it then click the **Open** button.

※ Make the changes you require in the template then click the 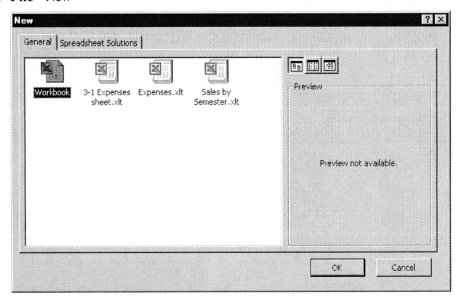 tool to save them.

※ Close the template.

3 ▪ Create a workbook based on a template

※ **File - New**

*The templates in the **Templates** folder appear in the **General** tab.*

※ If necessary, click the tab that corresponds to the folder that contains the template.

※ Double-click the template name.

When you open a template, Excel copies its contents into a new workbook; this workbook is given the name of the template followed by a number.

※ Enter data in the new workbook.

※ Save this new workbook as you would an ordinary workbook.

Below, you can see **Practice Exercise** 3.1. This exercise is made up of 3 steps. If you do not know how to complete one of the steps, go back to the lesson to refer to the corresponding title. When you have finished, check your work by reading the **Solution** on the next page.

All the steps in this exercise are likely to be tested in the exam.

Practice Exercise 3.1

1. Create a template called **Expenses.xlt** in which you should enter the following data:

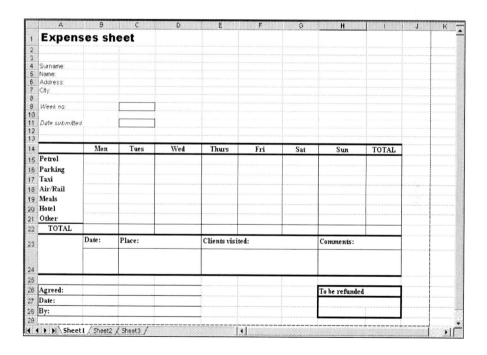

2. In the **3-1 Expenses sheet.xlt** template, make the following changes:
- put cells **B4** and **B5** in **bold**.
- apply the fill **Gray - 25%** to cells **I14** to **I21** and cells **B22** to **I22**.
The **3-1 Expenses sheet.xlt** template is found in the **Templates** folder (C:\Windows\Application Data\Microsoft\Templates).
Save the changes and close template **3-1 Expenses sheet.xlt**.

3. Create a new workbook based on the **3-1 Expenses sheet.xlt** template and complete the top of **Sheet1** as shown below:

	A	B	C	D
1	**Expenses sheet**			
2				
3				
4	Surname:	**ANDREWS**		
5	Name:	**Robin**		
6	Address:	55 Meadowside Wynd		
7	City:	Walker's Creek		
8				
9	Week no:		49	
10				
11	Date submitted:		11/01/00	
12				

Save this new workbook as **3-1 Expenses Andrews 49.xls** in the **MOUS Excel 2000 Expert** folder.

If you want to put what you have learned into practice in a real document, you can work on summary exercise 3 for the TEMPLATES, WORKBOOKS AND WORKGROUPS section that you can find at the end of this book.

It is often possible to perform a task in several different ways, but here only the quickest solution is presented. Go back to the lesson to see the other techniques that can be used.

Solution to Exercise 3.1

1. To create the Expenses.xlt template, create a new document by clicking the tool then enter and format the data below in **Sheet1** of the workbook.

	A	B	C	D	E	F	G	H	I	J	K
1	**Expenses sheet**										
2											
3											
4	Surname:										
5	Name:										
6	Address:										
7	City:										
8											
9	Week no:										
10											
11	Date submitted:										
12											
13											
14		Mon	Tues	Wed	Thurs	Fri	Sat	Sun	TOTAL		
15	Petrol										
16	Parking										
17	Taxi										
18	Air/Rail										
19	Meals										
20	Hotel										
21	Other										
22	TOTAL										
23		Date:	Place:		Clients visited:			Comments:			
24											
25											
26	Agreed:							To be refunded			
27	Date:										
28	By:										
29											

Sheet1 / Sheet2 / Sheet3 /

Use **File - Save As**.
Open the **Save as type** list and click the **Template (*.xlt)** option.
Type **Expenses** in the **File name** text box and click **Save**.

2. To make changes to the 3-1 Expenses sheet.xlt template in the Templates folder, use **File - Open**.
Open the **Look in** list, select drive **C** then double-click the **Windows**, **Application Data**, **Microsoft** and finally **Templates** folders.
Open the **Files of type** then select **Templates (*.xlt)**.
Select the template **3-1 Expenses sheet.xlt** then click **Open**.

To apply bold to cells B4 and B5, select cells **B4** and **B5** then click the **B** tool.

To apply the Gray - 25% fill to cells I15 to I21 and B22 to I22, select cells **I14** to **I21** and cells **B22** to **I22**.

Open the list associated with the tool and click **Gray - 25%**.

Click the tool then the button of the workbook window.

3. To create a new workbook based on the 3-1 Expenses sheet.xlt template, use **File - New**, double-click the icon of the **3-1 Expenses sheet.xlt** template and fill out the top part of **Sheet1** as shown in the screens illustrated on page 150.

To save this new workbook under 3-1 Expenses Andrews 49.xls, click the tool.
Open the **Save in** list, select the drive on which the **MOUS Excel 2000 Expert** folder has been copied then double-click the **MOUS Excel 2000 Expert** folder.
Make sure that the **Save as type** list is displaying **Microsoft Excel Workbook (*.xls)**.
Type **3-1 Expenses Andrews 49.xls** in the **File name** box then click **Save**.

TEMPLATES, WORKBOOKS AND WORKGROUPS
Lesson 3.2: Workbooks

TEMPLATES, WORKBOOKS AND WORKGROUPS
Lesson 3.2: Workbooks

1 ▪ Using the workspace

*It is possible to open several workbooks at once according to a preset page layout; to do this you would use a **workspace file**. In this file, information relative to the workbooks to be opened is stored, such as where they are saved, the size of the window, the position of the workbooks on the screen... but this file does not contain any workbooks.*

Creating a workspace file

▪ Open the workbooks that you want to group together in the workspace file.

▪ Resize and place the workbooks so that they appear as you want them to when you open the workspace file. To do this you can, for example, use the options in the **Window - Arrange** menu.

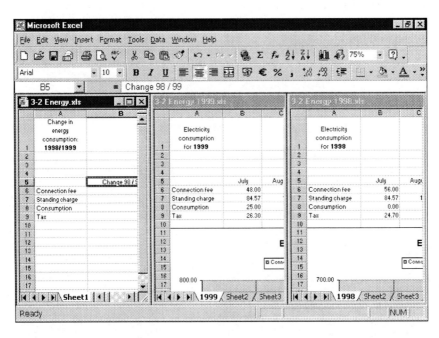

In this example, 3 workbooks are open and displayed vertically, side-by-side.

154

File - Save Workspace

*Notice that the **Save as type** box contains the choice **Workspaces (*.xlw)**.*

- Type the name of the file in the **File name** box. The .xlw extension is optional.

- Select the drive in which you want to save the workspace file.

- Click the **Save** button.

- If, for some workbooks in the group, changes made have not been saved, Excel asks if you want to do so: click **Yes** (or **Yes to All**) to save the changes and create the workspace file, click **No** to create the workspace file without saving the changes, or click **Cancel** if you do not want to create the workspace file.

Opening and closing a workspace file

- To open a workspace file, which means opening the workbooks that refer to the file, use **File - Open**.

- To close all the workbooks at the same time, hold down the ⌈Shift⌋ key and use **File - Close All**. You can also close the workbooks one by one using **File - Close** or by clicking the ☒ button in the workbook windows.

2 ▪ Linking workbooks

Workbooks are linked when a formula refers to one or more cells in another workbook.

- Open the workbook in which you want to create the calculation formula that is to refer to a cell in another workbook.

- Open the other workbook(s) that contain the cell(s) refered to.

You will see buttons on the taskbar that correspond to each open workbook.

- Activate the workbook that is to contain the formula by clicking the corresponding button on the taskbar.

*You can also use the **Window** menu and click the name of the workbook concerned.*

TEMPLATES, WORKBOOKS AND WORKGROUPS
Lesson 3.2: Workbooks

- Select the cell that is to contain the calculation formula.

- Type =.

- Create the formula as you would normally. When you refer to a cell in another workbook, show that workbook on the screen by clicking the corresponding button on the taskbar or by activating the appropriate option in the **Window** menu; then click the cell concerned.

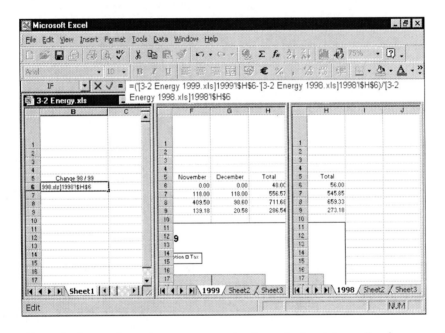

The calculation formula appears in the formula bar; the cell references that come from another workbook are preceded by the name of the sheet and the workbook.

- When you have finished the calculation formula, confirm by pressing ⏎.

When you open a workbook that contains a calculation formula with a link, you can choose to update the data.

⌨3 ▪ Changing the properties of a workbook

▪ Open the workbook concerned.

▪ **File - Properties**

▪ Click the **Summary** tab.

▪ Enter the information you want in the text boxes.

▪ Activate the **Save preview picture** option if you want Excel to save a picture of the first page of the file that will be displayed as a preview in the **Open** dialog box.

▪ Click **OK**.

▪ Remember to save the document.

 *The **Properties** command is unavailable if the structure of the workbook is protected against changes.*

*To change the properties of a workbook that is not open, use **File - Open** and select the file concerned. Click the **Tools** button then the **Properties** option.*

4 ▪ Creating a shared workbook

To allow several users on a network to work on the same workbook simultaneously, you must share it.

▫ Open the workbook that you want to share.

▫ **Tools - Share Workbook**

▫ Click the **Editing** tab.

▫ Activate the **Allow changes by more than one user at the same time** option.

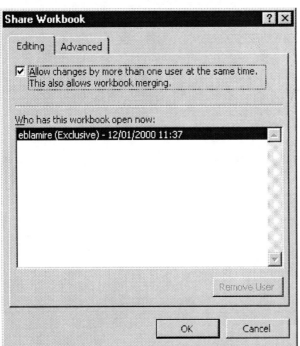

You can see the names of the users who are currently working with the workbook, in addition to the date and time they opened the workbook.

▫ Click **OK**.

▫ Excel asks you to save the workbook if you want to continue: click **OK**.

* If you have not already done so, you now need to make the shared workbook available to other users by saving it on the network where other users can access it. To do this, use **File - Save As**.

By doing this you make a copy of the shared workbook. The name of the workbook appears on the title bar, followed by the word **Shared**.

If you decide to change the workbook so that it is no longer shared, by deactivating the **Allow changes by more than one user at the same time** *option (* **Tools - Share Workbook - Editing** *tab), make sure that you are the only user in the* **Who has this workbook open now** *list. If this is not the case, the other users in the list will lose any work that has not been saved.*

 Using a shared workbook

* Open the workbook concerned.

You can add data, insert rows, columns, sort the data, but you cannot, for example, delete worksheets, define conditional formatting, merge cells, insert charts, objects or hyperlinks.

* To find out who the other users are, use **Tools - Share Workbook**, and click the **Editing** tab.

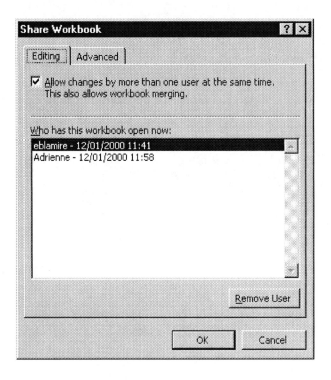

A list of current users is shown.

▦6 ▪ Merging workbooks

You can make copies of a shared workbook that can be used and changed independently by different users. These file copies can be merged in order to recreate a single file from the copies.

Copying a shared workbook

▪ Before making one or more copies of a shared folder which you intend to merge later, it is essential to prepare. To do this, use **Tools - Share Workbook**, and click the **Editing** tab.

▪ Tick the **Allow changes by more than one user at the same time** option.

▪ Click the **Advanced** tab.

※ Activate the **Keep change history for** option in the **Track changes** frame. In the **days** box, enter the number of days during which users can make changes and add comments to the shared workbook.

Be careful, you will not be able to merge copies of the workbook if this period is not observed. If there is any doubt about the date, enter a very high number of days, such as 1000.

※ Click **OK**.

※ To copy the workbook, use the **File - Save As** command and give a different name to each copy.

Merging workbooks

*The workbooks must be merged before the end of the period during which a history of any changes is kept (revision period). The length of this period is specified in the **Advanced** tab of **Tools - Share Workbook**.*

※ Open the shared workbook into which you want to merge changes from another workbook on the disk.

※ **Tools - Merge Workbooks**

※ If Excel asks you, save the workbook by clicking **OK**.

*The **Select Files to Merge Into Current Workbook** dialog box appears.*

※ *Select one or more copies of the shared workbook to be merged.*

To select several files, use the Shift *key to select adjacent files, or the* Ctrl *key for non-adjacent files.*

※ Click **OK** to merge the files.

🗎 *If you do not want to merge several copies of the shared workbook at the same time, you can use **Tools - Merge Workbooks** several times.*

Below, you can see **Practice Exercise** 3.2. This exercise is made up of 6 points. If you do not know to complete one of these steps, go back to the lesson to refer to the corresponding title. When you have finished, check your work by reading the **Solution** on the next page.

All the steps in this exercise are likely to be tested in the exam.

☞ Practice Exercise 3.2

1. Create a workspace file, called **Work**, and save it in the **MOUS Excel 2000 Expert** folder. This workspace file should open workbooks **3-2 Energy.xls**, **3-2 Energy 1999.xls** and **3-2 Energy 1998.xls**, all in the **MOUS Excel 2000 Expert** folder.
   When the **Work** workspace folder is opened, the three workbooks should all be displayed vertically on the screen.

2. Link the three files from the previous step by calculating the change in the energy consumption charges between 1998 and 1999. To do this, fill in cells **B6** to **B9** in the **3-2 Energy.xls** workbook.

3. Change the properties of the **3-2 Sport Base.xls** workbook in the **MOUS Excel 2000 Expert** folder as follows:

   Title: BSN Members

   Subject: List of basketball club members.

   Author: Kim Matheson

   Manager: Tim Robinson

   Category: Data list

   Keywords: sport

   Finally, you should save the preview picture.

4. Create a shared file using the **3-2 Sport base.xls** workbook that is saved in the **MOUS Excel 2000 Expert** folder. Save this shared workbook on a disk drive where other users can access it. To finish, close the workbook.

5. In the shared **3-2 Sport base.xls** workbook that you saved on the network in the last step, sort the **Name** column in ascending order.

6. Merge the **3-2 Shared1** and **3-2 Shared2** workbooks in the shared **3-2 Sport base merge.xls** workbook. These workbooks are in the **MOUS Excel 2000 Expert** folder; the **3-2 Shared1.xls** and **3-2 Shared2.xls** workbooks are copies of the **3-2 Sport Base merge.xls** workbook. Before carrying out this task, it would be a good idea to look at the changes made in workbooks **3-2 Shared1** and **3-2 Shared2** to make sure that:
   - in the **3-2 Shared1** workbook, the text in cell **C9** has been changed and that the characters in this cell are coloured red.
   - in the **3-2 Shared2** workbook, a row has been inserted between rows **5** and **6** in order to enter the information about Mary Henley.

If you want to put what you have learned into practice in a real document, you can work on summary exercise 3 for the TEMPLATES, WORKBOOKS AND WORKGROUPS section that you can find at the end of this book.

TEMPLATES, WORKBOOKS AND WORKGROUPS
Exercise 3.2: Workbooks

It is often possible to perform a task in several different ways, but here only the quickest solution is presented. Go back to the lesson to see the other techniques that can be used.

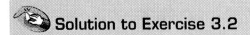 **Solution to Exercise 3.2**

1. To create the Work workspace, start by opening the three workbooks specified in the exercise, using **File - Open**. Change the display of the workbooks by using **Window - Arrange** command and activate the **Vertical** option before confirming with **OK**.

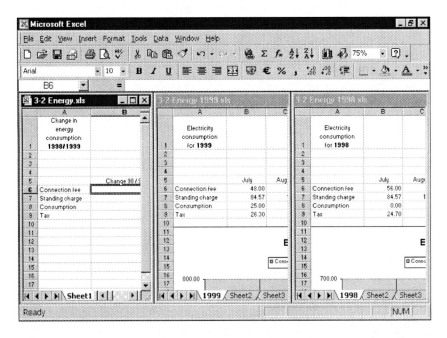

To save the workspace file, use **File - Save Workspace**, select the **MOUS Excel 2000 Expert** folder in the **Save in** list, type **Work** in the **File name** box and click **Save**.

To test this new file, close the three open workbooks, then use **File - Open**, select the **Work.xlw** file that is in the **MOUS Excel 2000 Expert** folder and click **Open**. The **3-2 Energy.xls**, **3-2 Energy 1998.xls** and **3-2 Energy 1999.xls** workbooks should open and appear vertically side-by-side.

2. To link the three workbooks using calculation formulas, click in cell **B6** in the **3-2 Energy.xls** workbook,
type =(
select cell **H6** in the **3-2 Energy 1999.xls** workbook,
type a minus sign **-**
select cell **H6** in the **3-2 Energy 1998.xls** workbook,
close the brackets by typing) followed by a dividing operator /
select cell **H6** in the **3-2 Energy 1998.xls** workbook.

The formula that appears in the formula bar should be:
=('[3-2 Energy 1999.xls]1999'!$H$6-'[3-2 Energy 1998.xls]1998'!$H$6)
/'[3-2 Energy 1998.xls]1998'!$H$6

Confirm by pressing ⏎.

Use the same technique for the calculation in cells **B7**, **B8** and **B9** in the **3-2 Energy.xls** workbook.

Here are the results:

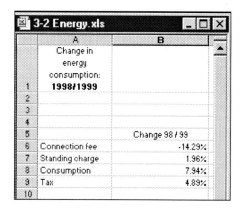

A percentage with 2 decimal places had been previously applied to the cells concerned.

For each of the workbooks, click the 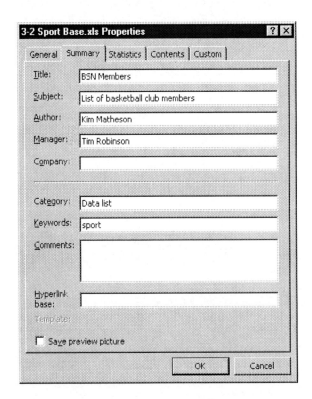 tool then the button in the workbook window.

3. To change the properties of the 3-2 Sport Base.xls workbook, open **3-2 Sport Base.xls** in the **MOUS Excel 2000 Expert** folder, use **File - Properties**, then click the **Summary** tab.
Enter the following information in the corresponding text boxes:

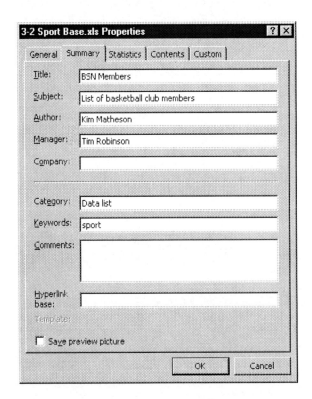

Activate the **Save preview picture** option then click **OK**.

4. To create a shared file using the 3-2 Sport Base.xls workbook, open, if necessary, **3-2 Sport Base.xls** from the **MOUS Excel 2000 Expert** folder. Run **Tools - Share Workbook** then click the **Editing** tab.

Activate the **Allow changes by more than one user at the same time** option, click **OK** and then **OK** again.

Save the shared workbook on a network so that it is available to other users. To do this, use **File - Save As**.

In the **Save in** list, select a drive on the disk that is accessible via a network connection then, if necessary, the folder in which the shared workbook is to be saved.

Click the **Save** button then the ⊠ button in the shared **3-2 Sport Base.xls** workbook window.

5. To sort the Name column in the shared workbook 3-2 Sport Base.xls by ascending order, open the **3-2 Sport Base.xls** shared workbook that you saved on the network during the previous step.

Click in cell **A2** then click ⟨↓⟩.

6. To merge the workbooks 3-2 Shared1 and 3-2 Shared2 in the shared workbook 3-2 Sport Base merge.xls, open **3-2 Sport Base merge.xls** in the **MOUS Excel 2000 Expert** folder and use **Tools - Merge Workbooks**.

In the **MOUS Excel 2000 Expert** folder, select workbooks **3-2 Shared1** and **3-2 Shared2** and click **OK**.

TEMPLATES, WORKBOOKS AND WORKGROUPS
Exercise 3.2: Workbooks

TEMPLATES, WORKBOOKS AND WORKGROUPS
Lesson 3.3: Tracking changes

1 ▪ Defining the frequency of updates in a shared workbook

Changes made by all the users of a shared workbook are updated automatically when the user saves the workbook. However, each user can change the options that specify the frequency at which he or she receives the modifications made by other users.

▪ Open the shared workbook.

▪ **Tools - Share Workbook**

▪ In the **Editing** tab, make sure that the **Allow changes by more than one user at the same time** option is active.

▪ Click the **Advanced** tab.

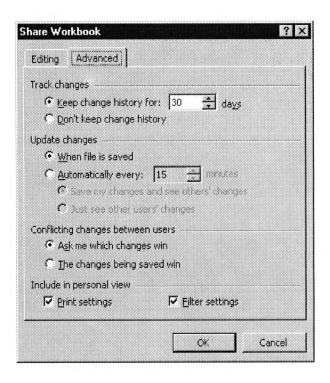

*In this dialog box, the **Update changes** frame is the area you should be looking at here.*

» Activate the **When file is saved** option to see changes made by other users each time the shared workbook is saved, or activate the **Automatically every** option and specify how often the workbook is to be updated in the **minutes** text box if you want regular updates of changes made by users.

If you have chosen the automatic update, use the following two options, to choose whether you want to **Save** (your) **changes and see others' changes**, or whether you want to **Just see other users' changes**.

» Click **OK**.

» Save the shared workbook.

2 ▪ Tracking changes in a shared workbook

In a shared workbook, this action will allow you to choose which changes you want to see and will highlight them.

» Open the shared workbook.

» **Tools - Track Changes - Highlight Changes**

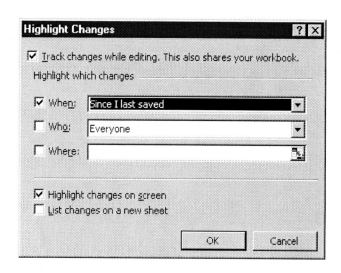

» Activate the **Track changes while editing** option.

*When this option is active, the options in the **Highlight which changes** frame are available and will allow you, if necessary, to specify the type of changes you want to highlight.*

» Activate the **When** option to highlight the changes that have been made during the time interval specified in this option's drop-down list.

Since I last saved	highlights only those changes made since the last time the workbook was saved.
All	highlights all the changes made to the workbook.
Not yet reviewed	highlights the changes that have not been accepted or rejected.
Since date...	highlights the changes made since the date entered in the **When** box.

» Activate the **Who** option and use the drop-down list to select the users whose changes you want to see.

» Activate the **Where** option and select the cell range in which you want to see the changes.

*If none of the options in the **Highlight which changes** frame are active, all the changes made to the shared workbook (yours and those made by other users) will be shown.*

» Activate the **Highlight changes on screen** option to highlight the changes. When you point to a highlighted cell, detailed information about that change will appear in a ScreenTip.

» Activate the **List changes on a new sheet** if you want to see the changes on a separate sheet; they will be listed on a worksheet called **History** and can be filtered.

» Click **OK**.

Microsoft Excel allocates a different colour to each user's changes.

You can also *highlight changes in a workbook that is not shared.*

▪ Accepting or rejecting changes in a shared workbook

Changes made can be accepted into the shared workbook or rejected. All the users of the shared workbook can do this.

* Open the shared workbook.

* **Tools - Track Changes - Accept or Reject Changes**

* If Excel asks you to save the workbook, click **OK**.

   *The **Select Changes to Accept or Reject** dialog box appears and will allow you to indicate which changes you want to review.*

* Activate the **When** option to review the changes made within the time interval selected in this option's drop-down list.

   Not yet reviewed   selects the changes that you have not yet reviewed.

   Since date...   reviews the changes made to the workbook since the date given in the **When** box.

* Activate the **Who** option and use the drop-down list to select the users whose changes you want to review.

* Activate the **Where** option then select the cell range in which you want to review the changes.

   If none of these options are active, all the changes made to the workbook will be reviewed.

* Click **OK**.

*The **Accept or Reject Changes** dialog box appears and the first change is highlighted in the workbook. You can see the details of the change in the dialog box.*

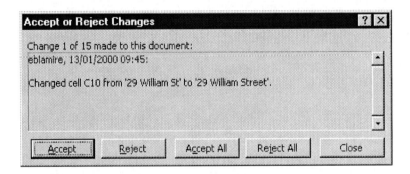

■ Click one of the following buttons:

Accept
to accept the change and remove the highlighting in the workbook.

Reject
to undo all the changes in the workbook.

Accept All
to accept all the changes in the workbook.

Reject All
to reject all the changes in the workbook.

Close
to close the dialog box and keep the changes that have been made.

■ If Excel asks you to select a value for a cell, click the value you want, then click **Accept**.

■ Repeat the above action for each change you review if you have not chosen to **Accept All** or **Reject All**.

 You can also accept or reject changes in a workbook that is not shared.

4 ▪ Solving conflicts in a shared workbook

When several users are working on the same file at the same time, it is possible that conflicts will arise when, for example, they change the contents of the same cell. This means that you need to decide how to deal with conflicting changes.

▪ Open the shared workbook.

▪ **Tools - Share Workbook**

▪ Click the **Advanced** tab.

▪ In the **Conflicting changes between users** frame, activate one of the following options:

Ask me which changes win	to review each conflicting change and decide which changes to keep when the workbook is saved.
The changes being saved win	to replace conflicting changes by your own when you save the shared workbook.

▪ Click **OK**.

▪ Save the shared workbook.

Below, you can see **Practice Exercise** 3.3. This exercise is made up of 4 points. If you do not know how to complete one of the steps, go back to the lesson to refer to the corresponding title. When you have finished, check your work by reading the **Solution** on the next page.

All the steps in this exercise are likely to be tested in the exam.

👉 **Practice Exercise 3.3**

In order to complete exercise 3.3 you should open **3-3 Sport Base.xls** in the **MOUS Excel 2000 Expert** folder.

1. Set the automatic update of the shared workbook to run every 30 minutes.

2. Highlight all the changes made by user **Adrienne** on the screen.

3. Accept all the changes that have not yet been reviewed, made by all the users, except the insertion of column **D** made by **Adrienne**.

4. For conflicting changes, replace them with your changes when you save the shared workbook.

If you want to put what you have learned into practice in a real document, you can work on summary exercise 3 for the TEMPLATES, WORKBOOKS AND WORKGROUPS section that you can find at the end of this book.

It is often possible to perform a task in several different ways, but here only the quickest solution is presented. Go back to the lesson to see the other techniques that can be used.

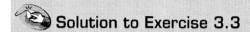 **Solution to Exercise 3.3**

⊞ 1. To set the frequency of automatic updates of the shared workbook to every 30 minutes, use **Tools - Share Workbook**, then click the **Advanced** tab. Activate the **Automatically every** option and enter **30** in the **minutes** box then click **OK**.

⊞ 2. To highlight all the changes made by user Adrienne on the screen, use **Tools - Track Changes - Highlight Changes**.
Open the drop-down list associated with the **When** option and click the **All** choice.
Open the drop-down list associated with the **Who** option and click the **Adrienne** choice.
Leave the **Highlight changes on screen** option active and click **OK**.

⊞ 3. To accept the changes made by all users that have not yet been reviewed, except the insertion of column D by user Adrienne, use **Tools - Track Changes - Accept or Reject Changes**.
Leave the **Not yet reviewed** choice selected in the **When** list.
Open the **Who** list, click the **Everyone** choice then click **OK**.
Click the **Accept** button twice and select **BROWN** in the list then click **Accept**. Select **Clare** in the list and click **Accept**. Click **Accept** 7 times and, finally, click **Reject** once.

4. To replace any conflicting changes with your own changes when you save the workbook, use **Tools - Share Workbook** and click the **Advanced** tab. Activate the **The changes being saved win** option in the **Conflicting changes between users** frame, then click **OK**.

TEMPLATES, WORKBOOKS AND WORKGROUPS
Lesson 3.4: Comments

1 ▪ Creating a comment

This technique allows you to add comments to cells and is particularly useful when used in workbooks that are shared between several users.

▪ Click in the cell to which you want to add the comment.

▪ **Insert - Comment** or 🔲 or ⌷Shift⌷ ⌷F2⌷

▪ Enter the text of the comment.

The comment is entered directly into a ScreenTip. You can go to the next line by pressing ⏎.

▪ Press ⌷Esc⌷ or click outside the ScreenTip when you have finished.

*In the top right corner of the cell, a little red triangle signals that the cell contains a comment. This indicator is visible if the corresponding option in the **Options** dialog box is active (**Tools - Options - View** tab); the comment remains visible if the **Comment & indicator** option is active.*

2 ▪ Viewing comments

▪ Simply point to the cell with the red triangle.

▪ If the comment indicator is not visible, use the buttons on the **Reviewing** toolbar:

    to scroll the comments in the worksheet.

    to show (or hide) all the comments.

3 ▪ Changing comments

* Click in the cell that contains the comment you want to change.
* **Insert - Edit Comment** or [image] on the **Reviewing** toolbar.
* Make the required changes in the ScreenTip.
* Press Esc or click outside of the ScreenTip when you have finished.

4 ▪ Deleting comments

* Click in the cell that contains the comment you want to delete.
* **Edit - Clear - Comments** or [image] on the **Reviewing** toolbar.

5 ▪ Printing comments

* View the comments that you want to print using the tools on the **Reviewing** toolbars:

   shows the comment in the active cell.

   shows all the comments in the active workbook.

* **File - Page Setup**
* Click the **Sheet** tab.
* Open the **Comments** list in the **Print** frame then select the **As displayed on sheet** choice to print the comments as they appear in the sheet, or the **At end of sheet** option to print the comments on a new page at the end of the document.
* Click **Print**.
* If necessary, select the relevant print options then click **OK**.

Below, you can see **Practice Exercise** 3.4. This exercise is made up of 5 steps. If you do not know how to complete one the steps, go back to the lesson to refer to the corresponding title. When you have finished, check your work by reading the **Solution** on the next page.

Steps that are likely to be tested in the exam are marked with a ⊞ symbol. It is however recommended that you follow the whole exercise in order to gain a complete understanding of the lesson.

☞ Practice Exercise 3.4

In order to complete exercise 3.4, you should open **3-4 Sport Base.xls** in the **MOUS Excel 2000 Expert** folder.

⊞ 1. Insert the following comments:
   - **"Reminder letter to be sent before 03/03/2000"** in cell **H1**.
   - **"Think about a new column to the left of column G for players' positions"** in cell **G1**.

2. View the comment in cell **A6**.

⊞ 3. Change the comment in cell **H1** as follows: **Reminder letter for payment of subs to be sent before 01/04/2000**.

⊞ 4. Delete the comment in cell **I1**.

5. Show then print all the comments as they appear in the worksheet.

If you want to put what you have learned into practice in a real document, you can work on summary exercise 3 for the TEMPLATES, WORKBOOKS AND WORKGROUPS section that you can find at the end of this book.

If is often possible to perform a task in several different ways, but here only the quickest solution is presented. Go back to the lesson to see the other techniques that can be used.

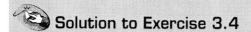 **Solution to Exercise 3.4**

1. To insert a comment in cell H1, click in cell **H1** then use **Insert - Comment**.
   Type **Reminder letter to be sent before 03/03/2000** then click outside the ScreenTip.

   To insert a comment in cell G1, click in cell **G1** then **Insert - Comment**.
   Type **Think about a new column to the left of column G for players' positions** then click outside the ScreenTip.

2. To see the comment in cell A6, point to cell **A6**.

3. To change the comment in cell H1, click in cell **H1** then **Insert - Edit Comment**.
   Change the text in the ScreenTip so that it reads **Reminder letter for payment of subs to be sent before 01/04/2000** then click outside the ScreenTip.

4. To delete the comment in cell G1, click in cell **G1** and use **Insert - Clear - Comments**.

5. To show all the comments, click the tool on the **Reviewing** toolbar.

To print all the comments as they appear in the worksheet, use **File - Page Setup**.

Under the **Sheet** tab, open the **Comments** list and choose the **As displayed on sheet** option.

Click **Print** and then **OK**.

TEMPLATES, WORKBOOKS AND WORKGROUPS
Lesson 3.5: Protection

1 ▪ Asking for a password when a workbook is opened

This operation allows you to define the password that will be requested when a workbook is opened and saved.

▪ Open the workbook concerned.

▪ **File - Save As**

▪ If necessary, enter the name of the document and specify where it is to be saved.

▪ Click the **Tools** button, then **General Options**.

▪ If you want to control who can open the workbook, enter a password in the **Password to open** text box.
If you want to stop those people who are not authorised to do so making changes to the workbook, enter a password in the **Password to modify** text box.

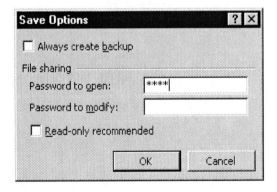

Asterisks replace the characters that you enter. Be very careful when using upper/lower case combinations, as Excel is case-sensitive.

▪ Click **OK**.

▪ Enter the **password** in the corresponding box to confirm then click **OK**.

▪ Click **Save** then **Yes** to save the changes.

📄 *Users must enter the password when they open the document; when a document is protected against changes, the **Read-only** button allows the user to open the document if they do not know the password but they will not be able to save any changes they make.*

📁2 ▪ Removing the password required to open a workbook

Only those people who know the password needed to open the workbook can remove it. In fact, this action requires you to open the workbook, so you need to know the password.

▪ **File - Open**

▪ Select the drive then the folder that contains the workbook concerned and double-click the workbook you want to open.

▪ Enter the workbook's **Password** in the corresponding text box then click **OK**.

▪ **File - Save As**

▪ Click the **Tools** button then click **General Options**.

▪ Select the asterisks in the appropriate text box then press ⌦Del.

▪ Click **OK**.

▪ Click the **Save** button then **Yes** to save the changes.

▤3 ▪ **Protecting the sheets in a workbook**

By protecting a workbook, you can prevent sheets from being deleted or moved, new sheets being added...

▪ Open the workbook concerned.

▪ **Tools - Protection - Protect Workbook**

▪ Make sure that the **Structure** option is active.

▪ Activate the **Windows** option to prevent the workbook window from being resized, moved, hidden or closed.

▪ If necessary, enter a **Password** (a maximum of 16 characters long) in the appropriate text box.

▪ Click **OK**.

▪ If necessary, re-enter the password then click **OK**.

▪ To cancel the protection of a workbook, use **Tools - Protection - Unprotect Workbook**.

▤4 ▪ **Protecting cells**

If you want to authorise data entry in certain cells only, you need to indicate in which cells data entry is authorised then protect the entire worksheet.

Unlocking cells

▪ Select the cells in which data entry is allowed.

▪ **Format - Cell** or ⌨ **1**

▪ In the **Protection** tab, deactivate the **Locked** option.

▪ Click **OK**.

Protecting the worksheet

- **Tools - Protection - Protect Sheet**

- Deactivate the options that you do want to protect in the **Protect worksheet for** frame.

- Enter a **Password** in the appropriate text box or simply click **OK** if you do not want to enter a password.

  You can enter up to 16 characters in the password. Be very careful, as Excel is case-sensitive. You will never see the characters on the screen.

- To confirm the password, re-enter it then click **OK**.

  If you try to enter data into a protected cell, the warning message below appears:

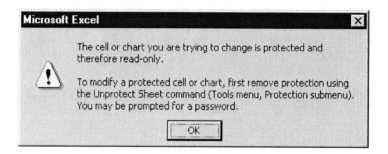

- Click **OK** to close this dialog box.

  *Some of the options in the **Format** menu are not available in a protected worksheet (the corresponding buttons appear grey).*

5 ▪ Removing protection (of a sheet or workbook)

▪ Open the workbook concerned.

▪ **Tools - Protection**

▪ Click the **Unprotect Workbook** option to cancel the protection of a whole workbook, or **Unprotect Worksheet** to cancel the protection of the active sheet.

▪ If necessary, enter the **Password** that protects the sheet or workbook.

▪ Click **OK**.

Below, you can see **Practice Exercise** 3.5. This exercise is made up of 5 steps. If you do not know how to complete one of the steps, go back to the lesson to refer to the corresponding title. When you have finished, check your work by reading the **Solution** on the next page.

All the steps in this exercise are likely to be tested in the exam.

☞ Practice Exercise 3.5

*In order to complete exercise 3.5 you should open **3-5 Hi-Fi.xls** in the **MOUS Excel 2000 Expert** folder.*

1. Control who can open **3-5 Hi-Fi.xls** by asking for the password **cama** (in lower case). Close the workbook.

2. Remove the password required to open **3-5 Hi-Fi.xls**.

3. Protect the structure of the sheets in **3-5 Hi-Fi.xls** as well as the workbook window with the password **renb** (in lower case).

4. Protect all the cells the **Turnover** worksheet in **3-5 Hi-Fi.xls** except cells **B8** to **D19** and cell **B26** in which data entry is authorised. Apply the password **pa2** in lower case to this protection.

5. Cancel the protection of the structure of the sheets and the workbook window for **3-5 Hi-Fi.xls**. Remember that the password is **renb** (in lower case).

If you want to put what you have learned into practice in a real document, you can work on summary exercise 3 for the TEMPLATES, WORKBOOKS AND WORKGROUPS section that you can find at the end of this book.

It is often possible to perform a task in several different ways, but here only the quickest solution is presented. Go back to the lesson to see the other techniques that can be used.

 Solution to Exercise 3.5

1. To control who can open 3-5 Hi-Fi.xls by asking for the password **cama**, use **File - Save As**.
   Click the **Tools** button, then the **General Options** choice.
   Click in the **Password to open** text box and type **cama** (in lower case) then click **OK**.
   Re-enter **cama** in the **Password** text box then click **OK**.
   Click **Save** and then **Yes**.

   To close 3-5 Hi-Fi.xls, click the ☒ button in the workbook window.

2. To remove the password required to open 3-5 Hi-Fi.xls, open the workbook, type **cama** (in lower case) in the **Password** text box then click **OK**.
   Use **File - Save As**, click the **Tools** button then choose **General Options**. Select the asterisks in the **Password to open** text box, press ⌨Del then click **OK**.
   Click **Save** and then **Yes**.

3. To protect the structure of the sheets and the workbook window in 3-5 Hi-Fi.xls, open, if necessary, **3-5 Hi-Fi.xls** then use **Tools - Protection - Protect Workbook**.
   Leave the **Structure** option active and activate the **Windows** option.
   Type **renb** in the **Password** text box and click **OK**.

   Re-enter **renb** in the **Password** text box then click **OK**.

4. To protect all the cells in the Turnover sheet in 3-5 Hi-Fi.xls, except cells B8 to D19 and cell B26, open **3-5 Hi-Fi.xls**, click the **Turnover** tab then select cells **B8** to **D19** and **B26**.
Use **Format - Cells**.
In the **Protection** tab, deactivate the **Locked** option then click **OK**.

Use **Tools - Protection** and click **Protect Sheet**.
Leave all three options under **Protect worksheet for**.
Type **pa2** (in lower case) in the **Password** text box and click **OK**.
Re-enter **pa2** in the **Password** box then click **OK**.

5. To remove the protection of the structure of the sheets and the window in 3-5 Hi-Fi.xls, open **3-5 Hi-Fi.xls** then use **Tools - Protection - Unprotect Workbook**.
Type **renb** in the **Password** text box then click **OK**.

PRINTING AND CONFIGURATION
Lesson 4.1: Printing

PRINTING AND CONFIGURATION
Lesson 4.1: Printing

1 ▪ **Printing and previewing several sheets**

▪ In the workbook, select the sheets that you want to preview and/or print: if they are adjacent, use the [Shift] key to select them; if not, hold the [Ctrl] key down as you click the corresponding tabs.

▪ To preview the selected sheets, use **File - Print Preview** or the [image] tool then display the next or preceding pages using the **Next** and **Previous** buttons or the [Page Down] and [Page Up] keys.

▪ To print the selected sheets, use **File - Print** or click the **Print** button in the preview window.
Define the print settings then click **OK** to print.

▪ Click an unselected tab to cancel the selection of the sheets.

📄 *You can also click the [image] tool, but if you do this, the sheets will be printed according to the current print settings.*

2 ▪ **Using views**

*A **view** allows you to save the current print area and the current page setup. When you activate a view, these settings are automatically activated.*

Creating a view

▪ Prepare the sheet for printing (page set up, print area, hiding columns…).

▪ **View - Custom Views**

▪ Click the **Add** button.

* Enter the **Name** of the view that you are creating.

* Indicate whether the view should include the **Print settings** and the **Hidden rows, columns and filter settings**.

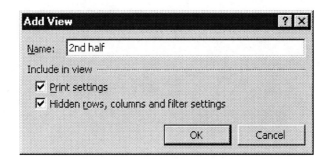

* Click **OK**.

Using views

* Open the workbook that contains the view you want to display.

* **View - Custom Views**

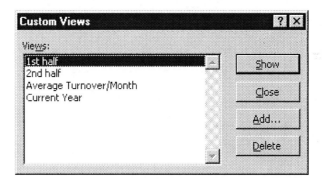

* Click the name of the view you want to see, in the **Views** list.

* Click **Show**.

Deleting a view

* Open the workbook that contains the view you want to delete.
* **View - Custom Views**
* In the **Views** list, click the name of the view you want to delete.
* Click the **Delete** button.

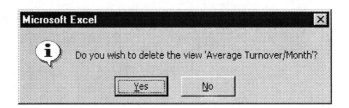

* Confirm the deletion by clicking **Yes**.
* Click the **Close** button.

🖷3 ▪ Creating a report

*A **report** allows you to print a set of views in a single document.*

* Create all the views you want to print successively.
* **View - Report Manager**

*If the **Report Manager** option is not in the menu, you need to install the corresponding Add-In.*

* Click **Add**.
* Give a name to the report in the **Report Name** text box.
* For each view you want to add to the report:
  - activate its name in the **View** list.
  - click **Add**.

The order in which you select the views determines the order in which they print them.

* If necessary, activate the **Continuous Page Numbers** option if you want pages to be numbered consecutively.

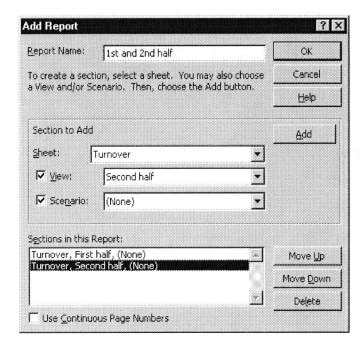

* If the print order is not what is required, you can change it in the **Sections in this Report** frame: click the view you want to move then use **Move Up** or **Move Down**.

* Click **OK**.

The report created is now available in the list of existing reports.

* Click **Close** to leave the **Report Manager** dialog box.

PRINTING AND CONFIGURATION
Lesson 4.1: Printing

▣ 4 ▪ Printing a report

※ **View - Report Manager**

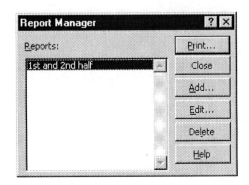

※ In the **Reports** list, click the report you want to print.

※ Click **Print**.

When you are printing a report, the number of options in the print options dialog box is much smaller.

※ Indicate the number of copies you want to print then click **OK**.

▣ 5 ▪ Managing existing reports

※ View - Report Manager

※ Click the name of the report in question in the **Reports** list.

※ Use the **Delete** or **Edit** buttons.

※ Finish by clicking **Close**.

Below, you can see **Practice Exercise** 4.1. This exercise is made up of 5 steps. If you do not know how to complete one of the steps, go back to the lesson to refer to the corresponding title. When you have finished, check your work by reading the **Solution** on the next page.

All the steps in this exercise are likely to be tested in the exam.

☞ Practice Exercise 4.1

*In order to complete exercise 4.1 you should open **4-1 Hi-Fi.xls** in the **MOUS Excel 2000 Expert** folder.*

1. Preview sheets **Stats** and **Turnover** and print two copies of each.

2. In the **Turnover** sheet, create the following views:
   - view **1st half** that displays only the turnover for January to June. To do this, you must hide rows **14** to **20**.
   - view **2nd half** that displays only the turnover for July to December. To do this, you will have to hide rows **8** to **13** and row **20**.
   This views should include the **Print settings** and the **Hidden rows, columns and filter settings**.
   Next, display view **Current Year** then delete the **Average Turnover/Month** view.

3. Create a report that will print views **1st half** and **2nd half**; call this report **1st and 2nd half** .

4. Print a copy of the **1st and 2nd half** report.

5. Change the print order of the views in **1st and 2nd half**. The **2nd half** view should precede the **1st half** view.

If you want to put what you have learned into practice in a real document, you can work on summary exercise 4 for the PRINTING AND CONFIGURATION section that you can find at the end of this book.

It is often possible to perform a task in several different ways, but here only the quickest solution is presented. Go back to the lesson to the see the other techniques that can be used.

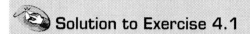

Solution to Exercise 4.1

1. To preview sheets Stats and Turnover, click the **Stats** tab, hold down the [Shift] key and click the **Turnover** tab.

   Click the ![tool] tool then use the **Next** and **Previous** buttons to scroll the pages.

   To print two copies of sheets Stats and Turnover, click **Print**.
   Leave the **Active sheet(s)** option active, type **2** in the **Number of copies** box and click **OK**.

   Click the **Sheet2** tab to cancel the selection of sheets **Stats** and **Turnover**.

2. To create the 1st half view in the Turnover sheet, which will display only the turnover for January to June, click the **Turnover** tab, select rows **14** to **20** then use **Format - Row - Hide**.

   Use **View - Custom Views** then click **Add**.
   Type **1st half** in the **Name** box, leave the **Print settings** and the **Hidden rows, columns and filter settings** options active then click **OK**.

   To create the 2nd half view in the Turnover sheet, which will display only the turnover for July to December, click the **Turnover** tab, select rows **13** to **21** then use **Format - Row - Unhide**.

   Select rows **8** to **13** and row **20** then use **Format - Row - Hide**.

   Use **View - Custom Views** then click **Add**.
   Type **2nd half** in the **Name** box, leave the **Print settings** and the **Hidden rows, columns and filter settings** options active then click **OK**.

To display the Current Year view, use **View - Custom Views**, click **Current Year** in the **Views** list then click **Show**.

To delete the Average Turnover/Month view, use **View - Custom Views**, select **Average Turnover/Month** in the **Views** list and click **Delete**. Click **Yes** to confirm the deletion then **Close**.

3. To create a report that will print the 1st half and 2nd half view, use **View - Report Manager** and click **Add**.
Type **1st and 2nd half** in the **Report Name** text box.
Select **1st half** in the **View** list and click **Add**.
Select **2nd half** in the **View** list and click **Add**.
Click **OK** then **Close**.

4. To print a copy of the 1st and 2nd half report, use **View - Report Manager**.
The **1st and 2nd half** report is already selected, so simply click **Print**.
Leave **1** in the **Copies** box and click **OK**.

5. To change the print order of the views in the 1st and 2nd half report, use **View - Report Manager**.
1st and 2nd half is already selected, so simply click **Edit**.
Click **Turnover, First half (None)** in the **Sections in this Report** list, then click the **Move Down** button.
Click **OK** then **Close**.

PRINTING AND CONFIGURATION
Lesson 4.2: Toolbars

1 ▪ **Showing/hiding a toolbar**

▪ **View - Toolbars**

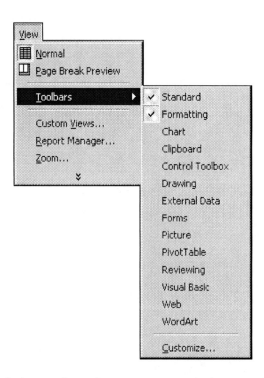

▪ Click the name of the toolbar that you want to show or hide, or click the **Customize** option to define which toolbar(s) you want to display; activate or deactivate the toolbars you want to show or hide then click **OK**.

 You can also right-click a toolbar then click the name of the toolbar you want to show or hide.

To show or hide the drawing toolbar, click the [icon] *tool.*

2 ▪ Creating a toolbar

* **View - Toolbars - Customize**
* Click the **Toolbars** tab.
* Click the **New** button.
* Give the **Toolbar name** in the appropriate zone then click **OK**.

  A small floating toolbar appears in the worksheet.
* To add the tools of your choice to the new toolbar, click the **Commands** tab. For each tool that you want to add, select the **Category** of the tool and drag the button in the **Commands** box from the dialog box to the new toolbar.
* Define the **Options** if necessary.
* Once all the tools have been added, click the **Close** button in the **Customize** dialog box.

3 ▪ Customising a toolbar

Deleting a tool

* Display the toolbar that contains the tool you want to delete.
* **View - Toolbars - Customize**
* Drag the tool you want to delete off the toolbar.

*As soon as you have removed the tool from the bar, it disappears. You can also carry out this action without opening the **Customize** dialog box: hold down the* 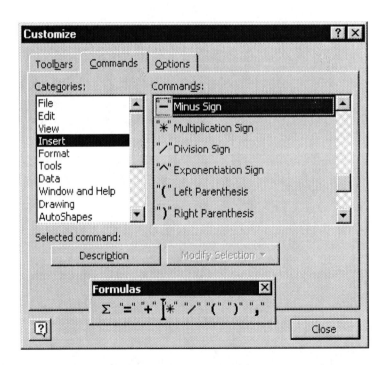 Alt *key and drag the tool off the bar.*

* If necessary, close the **Customize** dialog box by clicking **Close**.

Adding a tool

* **View - Toolbars - Customize**

* Click the **Commands** tab.

* In the **Categories** list, select the category of the tool you want to add.

* Drag the tool from the **Commands** box to the bar in question.

*The **Minus Sign** (-) tool will be added to the **Formulas** toolbar in the position of the vertical line.*

* If necessary, click **Close** in the **Customize** dialog box.

Clicking the ⟨⟩ symbol at the right end of some toolbars allows you to add or remove buttons.

Moving tools

» Display the toolbar that contains the tool you want to move.

» **View - Toolbars - Customize**

» Click in the toolbar in question, on the tool you want to move and drag it to its new position.

You can also carry out this action without opening the **Customize** dialog box: hold down the ⟨Alt⟩ key and drag the tool to its new position.

» If necessary, click **Close** to close the **Customize** dialog box.

After you change a toolbar, you can restore the original bar by clicking the **Restore** button in the **Customize** dialog box (**Toolbars** tab).

4 ▪ Assigning a macro with an action button

By clicking different buttons, you can rapidly carry out certain tasks. However, if the action associated with a button does not fit with your requirements, you can create your own macro and associate it with the button.

» If the button in question is already on a toolbar, display this bar.

» **View - Toolbars - Customize**

*You can also access this dialog box using **Tools - Customize**.*

- If the button with which you want to associate your macro is not on a toolbar, activate the **Commands** tab, click the **Category** required, select the button in question in the **Commands** box and drag it to one of the toolbars on the screen.

- In one of the toolbars on the screen, right-click the button with which you want to associate the macro.

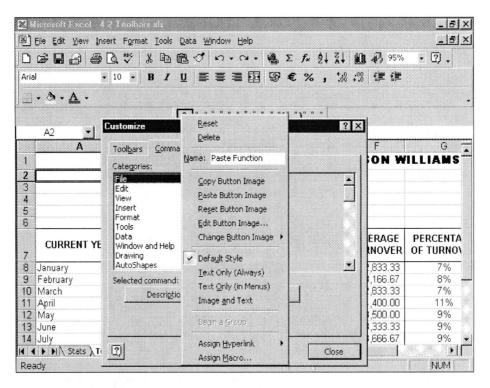

- Click the **Assign Macro** option.

- Select the macro that you want to assign to the button.

- Click **OK**.

- Click **Close** to close the **Customize** dialog box.

Below, you can see **Practice Exercise** 4.2. This exercise is made up of 4 steps. If you do not know how to complete one of the steps, go back to the lesson to refer to the corresponding title. When you have finished, check your work by reading the **Solution** on the next page.

Steps that are likely to be tested in the exam are marked with a ▦ symbol. It is however recommended that you follow the whole exercise in order to gain a complete understanding of the lesson.

☞ Practice Exercise 4.2

In order to complete exercise 4.2 you should open **4-2 Toolbars.xls** *in the* **MOUS Excel 2000 Expert** *folder and activate* **Turnover***; when you open the file, a message will ask you if you want to disable or enable the macros: click the* **Enable macros** *button.*

▦ 1. Show then hide the **Web** toolbar.

2. Create a **Formulas** toolbar and add the tools below:

▦ 3. In the **Formulas** toolbar, delete the ▦ then move the Σ tool to the end of the toolbar.

▦ 4. Assign the **DisplayFormulas** macro to the *fx* tool on the **Formulas** toolbar.

PRINTING AND CONFIGURATION
Exercise 4.2: Toolbars

If you want to put what you have learned into practice in a real document, you can work on summary exercise 4 for the PRINTING AND CONFIGURATION section that you can find at the end of this book.

It is often possible to perform a task in several different ways, but here only the quickest solution is presented. Go back to the lesson to see the other techniques that can be used.

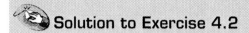 **Solution to Exercise 4.2**

1. To display the Web toolbar, right-click one of the toolbars on the screen then click the **Web** option.

   To hide the Web toolbar, right-click one of the toolbars on the screen then click the **Web** option again.

2. To create the Formulas toolbar, use **View - Toolbars - Customize** then click the **Toolbars** tab.
   Click the **New** button, type **Formulas** in the **Toolbar name** box then click **OK**.

   To add tools to the Formulas toolbars, click the **Commands** tab, then the **Insert** category.
   For each tool you want to add, select it in the **Commands** box and drag it to the **Formulas** toolbar in order to obtain the result below:

3. To delete the ⬚ tool from the Formulas toolbar, display the **Formulas** toolbar on the screen.

Hold down the ⬚Alt key, click the ⬚ tool and drag it off the **Formulas** toolbar.

To move the ⬚Σ tool to the end of the bar, hold the ⬚Alt key down, click the ⬚Σ tool and drag it to the end of the **Formulas** toolbar.

4. To assign the DisplayFormulas macro to the ⬚fx button on the Formulas toolbar, display the **Formulas** toolbar then use **View - Toolbars - Customize**.

Right-click the ⬚fx button on the **Formulas** toolbar then click the **Assign macro** option.
Select the **DisplayFormulas** macro then click **OK**.
Click **Close**.

MACROS
Lesson 5.1: Macros

MACROS
Lesson 5.1: Macros

📖 1 ▪ **Recording a macro**

- ※ If necessary, open the workbook in question.

- ※ **Tools - Macro - Record New Macro**

- ※ Type the name of the macro in the **Macro name** box.

- ※ Indicate, if necessary, the shortcut key that will run the macro.

- ※ Indicate where the macro should be recorded: in **This Workbook** (if the workbook is open) or in a **New Workbook.** If the macro is to be available all the time, choose **Personal Macro Workbook**.

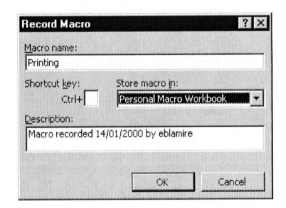

- ※ If necessary, enter text in the **Description** box to change or add to the information about the macro.

- ※ Click **OK**.

  *The macro toolbar (with two tools) appears as well as the word **Recording** on the status bar.*

- ※ Carry out all the actions you want to record in the macro.

- ※ Once all the actions have been completed, click the ▪ button on the macro toolbar (or **Tools - Macro - Stop Recording**).

Macros recorded in this way are created in a file called Personal.xls, which is where personal macros are stored. This workbook is opened automatically with Excel, which means these macros are always available.

⊞2 ▪ Running a macro

▪ If the macro was recorded in a workbook other than Personal.xls, open the workbook.

▪ Open the workbook in which you want to run the macro.

▪ **Tools - Macro - Macros** or ⎡ Alt ⎤⎡F8⎤

▪ Indicate where the macro you want to run is saved, using the **Macros in** list.

▪ Double-click the macro you want to run.

If the macro is in an open workbook or in Personal.xls, you can also use the shortcut key defined when the macro was recorded (if appropriate).

⊞3 ▪ Editing a macro

▪ If the macro is in Personal.xls, unhide this workbook using **Window - Unhide**.

▪ **Tools - Macro - Macros** or ⎡ Alt ⎤⎡F8⎤

▪ Select the macro in question then click **Edit**.

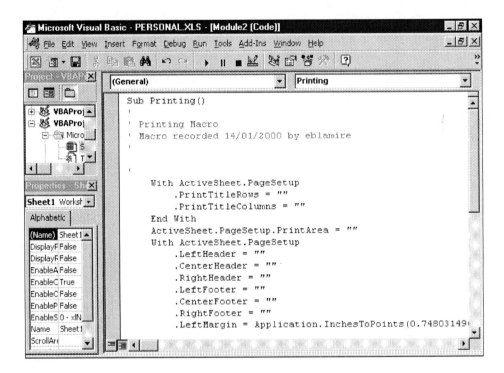

The contents of the macro appear in a Visual Basic window.

» Make the required changes.

» Click the ![save] tool to save the changes.

» Close the Visual Basic window by clicking the ![X] button or by **File - Close and return to Microsoft Excel**.

» If necessary, hide the **Personal.xls** workbook using **Window - Hide**.

Below, you can see **Practice Exercise** 5.1. This exercise is made up of 3 steps. If you do not know how to complete one of the steps, go back to the lesson to refer to the corresponding title. When you have finished, check your work by reading the **Solution** on the next page.

All the steps in this exercise are likely to be tested in the exam.

☞ Practice Exercise 5.1

1. In the **5-1 Exams.xls** workbook in the **MOUS Excel 2000 Expert** folder, create a macro called **Printing**. This macro will activate the **Landscape** page layout, reduce the scale to **95%** of normal size, centre the data **Horizontally** on the page and print two copies of the active sheets. This macro should be recorded in the **Personal Macro Workbook**, **Personal.xls** so that it can be used in any workbook.

2. Run the **Printing** macro in **5-1 HI-FI.xls** in the **MOUS Excel 2000 Expert** folder.
   This macro was recorded in the Personal.xls workbook.

3. In the **Printing** macro, change the zoom to **100%**.
   This macro was recorded in the Personal.xls workbook.

If you want to put what you have learned into practice in a real document, you can work on summary exercise 5 for the MACROS section that you can find at the end of this book.

It is often possible to perform a task in several different ways, but here only the quickest solution is presented. Go back to the lesson to see the other techniques that can be used.

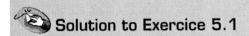

Solution to Exercice 5.1

1. To create the **Printing** macro in the 5-1 Exams.xls workbook, open **5-1 Exams.xls** in the **MOUS Excel 2000 Expert** folder then **Tools - Macro - Record New Macro**.
Type **Printing** in the **Macro name** box, select **Personal Macro Workbook** in the **Store macro in** list and click **OK**.

   Use **File - Page Setup** and in the **Page** tab, activate the **Landscape** option. Type **95** in the **Adjust to** box in the **Scaling** frame.

   Click the **Margins** tab, activate the **Horizontally** option in the **Center on page** frame then click **OK**.

   Run the **File-Print** command, leave the **Active Sheet(s)** option active, enter **2** in the **Number of copies** box then click **OK**.

   Click the ■ on the macro toolbar.

2. To run the Printing macro in 5-1 HI-FI.xls, open **5-1 HI-FI.xls** in the **MOUS Excel 2000 Expert** folder then **Tools - Macro - Macros**.
In the **Macros in** list, leave the **All Open Workbooks** option selected, and double-click the **PERSONAL.XLS!Printing** macro.

3. To change the zoom to 100% in the Printing macro that is recorded in the personal macro workbook Personal.xls, use **Window - Unhide** then click **OK**.

Use **Tools - Macro - Macros**, select the **Printing** macro and click **Edit**. Press `Ctrl` `Esc` to see the bottom of the window, select **95** in the .Zoom = 95 line and press `Del` then type **100**.

Click the button then **File - Close and Return to Microsoft Excel**.

Finish by hiding **Personal.xls** using **Window - Hide**.

MACROS
Exercise 5.1: Macros

SUMMARY EXERCISES

Summary exercise 1   MANAGING DATA

Open the **VALLEY LTD.xls** workbook in the **Summary** folder in the **MOUS Excel 2000 Expert** folder.

In the **Customer list** worksheet, import all the data in the **Valley ltd customer base.txt** file that is stored in the **Summary** folder of the **MOUS Excel 2000 Expert** folder (the first destination cell is cell A1): the source data are delimited, the separator is a tab stop and the column format is general. Once you have copied the data, adjust the width of columns **A** to **G**.

Name the cell range **A1** to **G52 customers**.

In cells D5, D6 and D7 of the **Invoice** worksheet, enter a formula that will automatically display the name, address and city that correspond to the code entered in cell **B10**; the data concerning the customers are in the **Customer list** worksheet.

Apply a comma format, with no decimal places, to cells B9 to F27 in the **Report** worksheet.

Use conditional formatting in cells B27 to E27 to show annual totals greater than or equal to 150000 in red.

Create an automatic outline of the table in the **Report** worksheet then use this outline to display only the results shown on the screen below:

Fruits / This year	FRUIT PRODUCTION				TOTAL
	Golden Delicious	Williams Pears	Bananas	Nectarines	
1st Semester	96,200	113,350	76,270	8,610	**294,430**
July	13,000	18,000	10,000	8,600	**49,600**
August	14,900	18,200	11,500	16,000	**60,600**
September	15,000	18,300	10,000	22,000	**65,300**
3rd Quarter	42,900	54,500	31,500	46,600	**175,500**
4th Quarter	68,240	67,630	24,140	25,080	**185,090**
2nd Semester	111,140	122,130	55,640	71,680	**360,590**
ANNUAL TOTAL	207,340	235,480	**131,910**	**80,290**	**655,020**

The following changes need to made in the **Customer list** worksheet, using the data form:

- Mrs CHEYNE is no longer a customer: delete her record.

- Mr MOORE has moved: enter his new address "38 Medway Grove".

Filter the data list in the **Customer list** worksheet in order to display only male customers from the **Three Rivers** and **Mapleton** districts.

Display all the records then sort the list by district, then by city and finally by name.

SUMMARY EXERCISES

From the data list in the **Customer list** worksheet, display different selections in order to achieve the result below:

List of women in Redfern

Title	Name	Address	City	Postcode
Mrs	NICHOLLS	33 Ridley Street	Rafter	6250
Miss	PIXTON	44 Clerk Street	Rafter	6250
Mrs	STOTT	78 Red Street	Rafter	6250

List of female customers from Mapleton and of all customers from Port Free and Herston

Title	Name	Address	City	Postcode	District
Mr	ADAMS	30 Lakeside	Port Free	6530	Dolphin Bay
Miss	FAIRCHILDE	103 Westwood Avenue	Port Free	6530	Dolphin Bay
Mrs	HENREY	30 Meadow Lane	Port Free	6530	Dolphin Bay
Mr	JONES	14 Lakeside	Port Free	6530	Dolphin Bay
Mr	MOORE	38 Medway Grove	Port Free	6530	Dolphin Bay
Miss	CRAMMOND	45 Bethel Rise	Herston	4150	Mapleton
Miss	JONES	39 Blackfriar's Drive	Herston	4150	Mapleton
Mr	LANGLEY	26 Field Lane	Herston	4150	Mapleton
Mr	MAXWELL	89 Peel Place	Herston	4150	Mapleton
Mr	MAXWELL	11 Forest Rise	Herston	4150	Mapleton
Mrs	PARK	55 Tulip Avenue	Herston	4150	Mapleton

In the **Customer list** worksheet, apply validation criteria to cells **B2** to **B100** of the **Title** column. The data **Miss**, **Mrs** and **Mr** should be in a drop-down list.

Finally, in the data list in the **Customer list** worksheet, enter lines of statistics that will show the number of customers per district.

A solution is saved under the name **Solution 1.xls** in the **Summary** folder.

Open the **TEMPO & CO.xls** workbook that is in the **Summary** folder in the **MOUS Excel 2000 Expert** folder.

Display the **Auditing** toolbar, then use the auditing arrows to find the precedents of cell **L4** and the dependents of cell **F5** in the **Employee list** worksheet.

In the **Employee list** worksheet, define what the value of cell **G10** (Amy MOFFAT's gross salary) should be in order for the gross total in cell **L10** to equal **1500**.

From the data list in the **Employee list** worksheet, use pivot table tools to obtain the table below:

SURNAME	(All)		
Sum of GROSS□TOTAL	NIGHT□WORK		
JOB□DESCRIPTION	N	Y	Grand Total
Accountant	7890		7890
Janitor		1090	1090
Mechanic		2340	2340
Office manager	1210		1210
Production manager	1400	4460	5860
Receptionist		1140	1140
Secretary	3505		3505
Supervisor	2665	4105	6770
Technician	3310	1240	4550
Typist	2330	1170	3500
Grand Total	22310	15545	37855

This new pivot table should be inserted in a new sheet that should be called **Analysis** and should be independent of the existing pivot table in the **Pivot table** worksheet.

Change the pivot table so that the **Production manager** and **Supervisor** jobs are no longer shown, then apply AutoFormat **Table 10**.

In the **Pivot table** worksheet, group the elements of the **ID CODE** field by tens.

In a chart sheet that should be called **Chart Analysis**, create the pivot chart associated with the pivot table in the **Analysis** worksheet. Modify the chart type to obtain the pivot chart below:

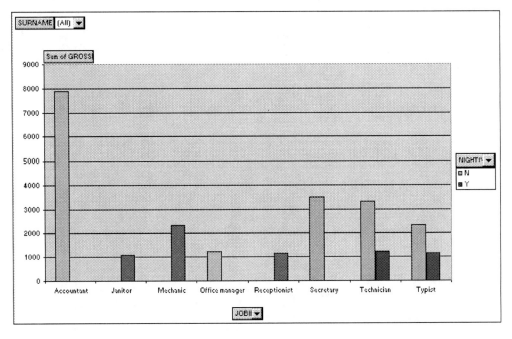

A solution is saved under the name **Solution 2.xls** in the **Summary** folder.

Summary exercise 3

WORKBOOKS, TEMPLATES AND WORKGROUPS

Change the **Sales by Semester.xlt** template so that cells **B6** to **D6** and **A8** to **A15** have a **Gray - 25%** fill. Save and close the template.

Create a workbook based on the **Sales by Semester.xlt** template and complete it as shown below:

SALES ANALYSIS BY SEMESTER

1st Semester

LIST OF SALES PEOPLE	JANUARY	FEBRUARY	MARCH	TOTAL	BONUS
PETER	4,568.90	3,958.00	4,578.50	13,105.40	196.58
CALLUM	2,587.00	3,250.00	2,356.00	8,193.00	
SUE	6,589.10	3,845.00	4,578.90	15,013.00	300.26
JOSH	6,348.00	7,890.00	7,845.10	22,083.10	662.49
ANNE	2,890.00	4,560.00	3,589.00	11,039.00	165.59
WENDY	4,578.90	7,125.00	4,560.00	16,263.90	325.28
BEN	3,875.00	4,500.00	5,230.00	13,605.00	204.08
PHILIP	4,580.00	5,845.00	2,356.00	12,781.00	191.72
TOTAL	36,016.90	40,973.00	35,093.50	112,083.40	2,045.99
AVERAGE	4,502.11	5,121.63	4,386.69	14,010.43	292.28
MINIMUM SALES	2,587.00	3,250.00	2,356.00	8,193.00	165.59
MAXIMUM SALES	6,589.10	7,890.00	7,845.10	22,083.10	662.49

Save the workbook as **Sales Semester1.xls** in the **Summary** folder of the **MOUS Excel 2000 Expert** folder.

SUMMARY EXERCISES

Change the properties of the workbook as shown below:

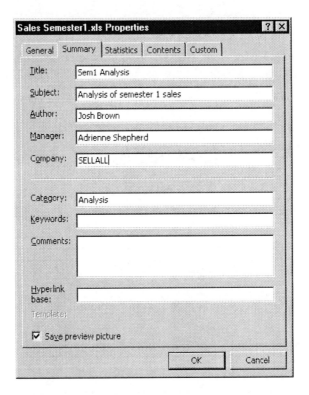

Create the following comments:

- **"sales person recruited at the beginning of January"** in cell **A9**.

- **"clear improvement compared with the last semester of previous year"** in cell **A13**.

Protect all the cells in **Sheet1** except cells **A6** to **D15**, in which data can be entered. Add the password **sem1** (in lower case) to this protection.

Print **Sheet1** with its comments, which should be printed on a separate page.

A solution is saved under the name **Solution 3.xls** in the **Summary** folder.

Summary exercise 4   PRINTING AND CONFIGURATION

Open the **Vehicles.xls** workbook stored in the **Summary** folder of the **MOUS Excel 2000 Expert** folder.

Preview the **Details** and **Overview - Year** sheets then print two copies of them.

In the **Details** sheet, create the following views:

- **West Valley** view, displaying only the number of vehicles constructed in the factories in **West Valley**. To do this you will need to hide rows **12** to **23**.

- **summary** view, displaying only the totals and percentages for each factory. To do this you will need to hide columns **B** to **E**.
  Next show the **Current** view in order to see the whole table again.

Create a report that will allow you to print views **Northern Peninsula**, **Walker Bay** and **West Valley**; this report should be called **Regions**.
Now print the **Regions** report.

Create a **Rows/columns/cells** toolbar and add the tools below (naturally, this toolbar cannot be included in the solution):

A solution is saved under the name **Solution 4.xls** in the **Summary** folder.

SUMMARY EXERCISES

Summary exercise 5   MACROS

In a new workbook, create a macro called **Print_formulas**. This macro should be saved in the **Personal Macro Workbook (Personal.xls)** and when it runs should:

- show formulas instead of values in the worksheet; to do this, use **Tools - Options - View** tab.

- use **Landscape** page orientation.

- print the gridlines and the row and column headers.

- print the workbook name in the right of the header and the page number in the middle of the footer.

- print two copies of the selected sheets (when the message 'Microsoft Excel did not find anything to print' appears, click OK).

Open the **Due Date.xls** workbook and run the **Print_formulas** macro.

Microsoft Excel 2000 Expert Table of objectives 🪟				
Task	**Lesson**	**Page**	**Exercise**	**Page**
Importing and exporting data				
Import data from text files (insert, drag and drop)	Lesson 1.2 Title 1	22	Exercise 1.2 Point 1	40
Import from other applications	Lesson 1.2 Title 2	25	Exercise 1.2 Point 2	40
Import a table from an HTML file (insert, drag and drop - including HTML round tripping)	Lesson 1.2 Title 3	29	Exercise 1.2 Point 3	40
Export to other applications	Lesson 1.2 Title 4	34	Exercise 1.2 Point 4	40
Using templates				
Apply templates	Lesson 3.1 Title 3	148	Exercise 3.1 Point 3	150
Edit templates	Lesson 3.1 Title 2	147	Exercise 3.1 Point 2	150
Create templates	Lesson 3.1 Title 1	146	Exercise 3.1 Point 1	149
Using multiple workbooks				
Using a workspace	Lesson 3.2 Title 1	154	Exercise 3.2 Point 1	162
Link workbooks	Lesson 3.2 Title 2	155	Exercise 3.2 Point 2	162
Formatting numbers				
Apply number formats (accounting, currency, number)	Lesson 1.3 Title 1	44	Exercise 1.3 Point 1	48
Create custom number formats	Lesson 1.3 Title 2	45	Exercise 1.3 Point 2	48
Use conditional formatting	Lesson 1.3 Title 3	46	Exercise 1.3 Point 3	48

TABLE OF OBJECTIVES

Task	Lesson	Page	Exercise	Page
Printing workbooks				
Print and preview multiple worksheets	Lesson 4.1 Title 1	196	Exercise 4.1 Point 1	201
Use the Report Manager	Lesson 4.1 Titles 2, 3, 4 and 5	196 to 200	Exercise 4.1 Points 2, 3, 4 and 5	201 and 202
Working with named ranges				
Add and delete a named range	Lesson 1.1 Titles 1 and 2	12 and 13	Exercise 1.1 Points 1 and 2	18
Use a named range in a formula	Lesson 1.1 Title 3	14	Exercise 1.1 Point 3	18
Use Lookup Functions (Hlookup or Vlookup)	Lesson 1.1 Title 4	15	Exercise 1.1 Point 4	18
Working with toolbars				
Hide and display toolbars	Lesson 4.2 Title 1	206	Exercise 4.2 Point 1	211
Customize a toolbar	Lesson 4.2 Title 3	207	Exercise 4.2 Point 3	211
Assign a macro to a command button	Lesson 4.2 Title 4	209	Exercise 4.2 Point 4	211
Using macros				
Record macros	Lesson 5.1 Title 1	216	Exercise 5.1 Point 1	219
Run macros	Lesson 5.1 Title 2	217	Exercise 5.1 Point 2	219
Edit macros	Lesson 5.1 Title 3	217	Exercise 5.1 Point 3	219
Auditing a worksheet				
Work with the Auditing Toolbar	Lesson 2.1 Title 1	90	Exercise 2.1 Point 1	95
Trace errors (find and fix errors)	Lesson 2.1 Title 2	90	Exercise 2.1 Point 2	95

Task	Lesson	Page	Exercise	Page
Trace precedents (find cells referred to in a specific formula)	Lesson 2.1 Title 4	92	Exercise 2.1 Point 4	95
Trace dependents (find formulas that refer to a specific cell)	Lesson 2.1 Title 3	91	Exercise 2.1 Point 3	95
Displaying and Formatting Data				
Apply conditional formats	Lesson 1.3 Title 3	46	Exercise 1.3 Point 3	48
Perform single and multi-level sorts	Lesson 1.5 Title 7	71	Exercise 1.5 Point 7	84
Use grouping and outlines	Lesson 1.4 Titles 1, 2 and 3	52 to 55	Exercise 1.4 Points 1, 2 and 3	57
Use data forms	Lesson 1.5 Title 1	60	Exercise 1.5 Point 1	83
Use subtotaling	Lesson 1.4 Title 4	55	Exercise 1.4 Point 4	57
Apply data filters	Lesson 1.5 Titles 2, 3, 4 and 5	65 to 70	Exercise 1.5 Points 2, 3, 4 and 5	83
Extract data	Lesson 1.5 Title 6	70	Exercise 1.5 Point 6	84
Query databases	Lesson 1.5 Title 10	76	Exercise 1.5 Point 10	84
Use data validation	Lesson 1.5 Titles 8 and 9	72 to 75	Exercise 1.5 Points 8 and 9	84
Using analysis tools				
Use PivotTable autoformat	Lesson 2.3 Title 3	116	Exercise 2.3 Point 3	128
Use Goal Seek	Lesson 2.2 Title 1	98	Exercise 2.2 Point 1	104
Create pivot chart reports	Lesson 2.4 Title 1	136	Exercise 2.4 Point 1	140
Work with Scenarios	Lesson 2.2 Title 4	102	Exercise 2.2 Point 4	104
Use Solver	Lesson 2.2 Titles 2 and 3	99 to 101	Exercise 2.2 Points 2 and 3	104

TABLE OF OBJECTIVES

Task	Lesson	Page	Exercise	Page
Use data analysis and PivotTables	Lesson 2.1 Title 5	94	Exercise 2.1 Point 5	95
	Lesson 2.3 Titles 1, 2 and 4	112 to 114 and 117	Exercise 2.3 Points 1, 2 and 4	127 and 128
Create interactive PivotTables for the Web	Lesson 2.3 Title 5	118	Exercise 2.3 Point 5	128
Add fields to a PivotTable using the Web browser	Lesson 2.3 Title 6	121	Exercise 2.3 Point 6	128
Collaborating with workgroups				
Create, edit and remove a comment	Lesson 3.4 Titles 1, 3 and 4	180 and 181	Exercise 3.4 Points 1, 3 and 4	182
Apply and remove worksheet and workbook protection	Lesson 3.5 Titles 3, 4 and 5	188 to 190	Exercise 3.5 Points 3, 4 and 5	191
Change workbook properties	Lesson 3.2 Title 3	157	Exercise 3.2 Point 3	162
Apply and remove file passwords	Lesson 3.5 Titles 1 and 2	186 to 187	Exercise 3.5 Points 1 and 2	191
Track changes (highlight, accept, and reject)	Lesson 3.3 Titles 1, 2, 3 and 4	170 to 175	Exercise 3.3 Points 1, 2, 3 and 4	176
Create a shared workbook	Lesson 3.2 Titles 4 and 5	158 and 159	Exercise 3.2 Points 4 and 5	163
Merge workbooks	Lesson 3.2 Title 6	160	Exercise 3.2 Point 6	163

A

ANALYSING

Data 94

APPLICATION

Exporting data to other
applications 34
Importing data from
other applications 25
Inserting a workbook into
another application as an object 38

AUDITING

Showing dependents 91
Showing errors 90
Showing precedents 92
Showing/hiding the toolbar 90

C

CALCULATION

Inserting rows of statistics 55

CELL

See also NAME

CHANGES

Accepting/rejecting 173
Defining the frequency
of updates 170
Highlighting 171
Solving conflicts in a shared
workbook 175

COMMENTS

Changing 181
Creating 180
Deleting 181
Printing 181
Viewing 180

COPYING

Exporting data to other
applications 36
Importing data from
other applications 25

CRITERIA

Defining validation criteria 72
Sorting a table 71
See also LIST OF DATA

D

DATA LIST

See LIST OF DATA

INDEX

H

HTML

I

IMPORTING

L

LINK

LIST OF DATA

LOCKING

LOOKUP

M

MACROS

List of available titles in
the Microsoft Office User Specialist collection

Visit our Internet site for the list of the latest titles published.
http://www.eni-publishing.com

ACCESS 2000
EXCEL 2000 CORE
EXCEL 2000 EXPERT
EXCEL 2002 EXPERT
OUTLOOK 2000
POWERPOINT 2000
WORD 2000 CORE
WORD 2000 EXPERT
WORD 2002 EXPERT